The Moon Carrier

One Hundred Poems about
Love, Romance and Tea

Words by
Ian Rowland

Illustrations by
Francesca DeWinter

Publication

The Moon Carrier

by Ian Rowland
Illustrations by Francesca DeWinter

Second edition

Published by Ian Rowland Limited

Ian's Dedication

I dedicate this book to all those who, one way or another,
provided the material, stories and inspiration for it. I also dedicate
it to everyone brave enough to discover that love is what makes
everything else make sense. And to everyone that likes tea.

Francesca's Dedication

To Eve, for being my harshest but most honest critic. To Vienna,
for laughing in all the right places and some of the wrong ones.
And to my husband, whose shoulders are broader and stronger
than anything I could ever draw.

A Quick Note About Me

I do three things so I have three websites.

www.ianrowland.com

This is about my work as a professional freelance writer. In simple terms, I offer a complete 'start-to-finish' writing and publishing service. Technical writing, business, sales, creative... you name it, I've done it! I offer about 40 years professional experience. In my career, I've helped more companies to sell a greater range of goods and services than anyone else you're likely to meet. I'm also a 'ghostwriter'! If you've got a book inside you, I can write it for you or guide you through the self-publishing process.

www.coldreadingsuccess.com

My website devoted to the art, science and joy of cold reading and what I call 'cold reading for business'. As well as providing free information and downloads, the site tells you about my three books on cold reading and the training I offer.

www.ianrowlandtraining.com

All about my talks and training for conferences, corporate groups and private clients. Main subjects include:

- The Practical Persuasion Method.
- Creative Problem-Solving.
- Leadership, Presence And Charisma.
- Unlock Your Mind.
- Cold Reading For Business.

I also offer bespoke training packages to suit your needs. Clients to date include the FBI, Google, Coca-Cola, Unilever, the Ministry Of Defence, the British Olympics Team, the Crown Estate and many more. Full details on the site.

Introduction

Ever since I was a young child, I've been familiar with the expression 'it's neither use nor ornament'. In the north-west of England, where I grew up, this is a common way to describe something that seems to serve no purpose. In my view, it's the perfect way to describe this book.

This collection of verse I've scribbled over the years doesn't have a purpose and I won't pretend otherwise. I wrote this book because I wanted to and because it wanted — in fact, *demanded* — to be written. That's all there is to it.

Life has been extraordinarily and magically kind to me. The kindest part of all is that, among all my travels, adventures, lessons, laughter and bruises, I've been able to learn what we all learn eventually: love is what makes everything else make sense.

— Ian Rowland

London, 2021

A Note About The Layout

In this book, I did the words and Francesca did the art. Francesca had some input regarding the layout, particularly where this became a little complicated (e.g. 'Male Order Pride' and 'More Likely'). However, most of the layout is down to me. Where the layout is good you can credit Francesca and where it isn't you can blame me.

Contents

The Moon Carrier

Can I win her hand, her morning embrace?
  As much chance as from your own shadow escape
  So laughed they all, so laughed they all

Can I kiss her lips, her cheek and her breast?
  As much chance as halt time for one hour's rest
  So laughed they all, so laughed they all

Can I share her passion in sun-scented rooms?
  As much chance as in your hands carry the moon
  So laughed they all, so laughed they all

    But true to my dream was I
    True to the girl with raven hair
    And true to my hope was I
    True to the girl with heart to share

So choosing the dusk of a moonless night
I ran to the hills and there at my side
My shadow did run but as the sunlight
Disappeared so faded his shape and his stride

Then choosing a day of sun's fierce glare
I came to the sundial set in the square
Which, wrenched from its base, I did slowly rotate
So that time, for one hour, kept motionless state

Then choosing the eve of brightest full moon
Its image reclined on a freshwater pool
With hands cupped I raised that silvery jewel
So witnessed they all, and each one a fool

> Thus true to my dream was I
> True to the girl with raven hair
> And true to my hope was I
> True to the girl with heart to share
>
> Who shared her heart with…
> Her Moon Carrier

Here Is The News

Here is the news ten years from now
Still few signs of flying cows
Foldable buildings: not many planned
Finnish agoraphobics: not many tanned
In economic terms it's a bit of a mess
(Though rich folk feel it rather less)
Politicians gave a speech or two
That were mainly 'Blah blah policy review'
While scientists failed to create what they oughta:
A flying car that runs on water

The weather was dry or wet or a mix
While the Nobel Prize for new card tricks
Was not awarded again today
At a big ceremony that didn't take place
In sport some team somewhere won a cup
Another team lost and cursed their luck
Traffic in cities got quite congested
Clumsy thieves got quite arrested
Chocolate bars got quite ingested
"Rhymes getting worse", a critic suggested

Rabbits still good at making rabbits
Bears in woods: no change in habits
Boa constrictors still will strangle ya
Spiders' webs still not triangular
In business news: some up, some down
In tidal news: some in, some out
Time travel still not widely available
Knitted umbrellas still not very sale-able
Ten years hence, what else ain't new?
I still haven't got anywhere with you…

When It's Gone

What is love like when it's gone?
Like a web that wasn't spun
Like a shine that never shone
Like a wand that's only wan

Like a lover lacking L
Like a storm without a quell
Like the wish that isn't well
Like the sold without the sell

Like someone took the 'f' from 'fun'
Like the music of bar none
Like the ending not begun
Like all eclipse and never sun

Like the sex without the 's'
Like the page without the press
Like the end without the less
Like the suc- without the -cess

Like a truce without a true
Like the old was never new
Like a do that's never done
Like the prize…
           …is to be one

Male Order Pride

Dear Sirs, please find me a partner
As honest as honest can be
A women I'll always be able to trust
With values and integrity

> *Dear Sir, that's no problem at all*
> *We'll send you a woman at once*
> *Sister Gertude de Angelus*
> *As honest as ever there was*

Dear Sirs, meaning no disrespect
She has to be honest… but fun
A woman who knows how to let her hair down
In ways not typically nun

> *Dear Sir, we'll try to combine*
> *Your wishes as best we may*
> *We've Borise, the Russian shot-putter*
> *Who's a whole ton of fun, in her way*

Dear Sirs, I neglected to specify
Pretty and feminine too
I'm returning the pic of Borise, P.S.
Was that the front or rear view?

Dear Sir, if looks are important
Then let all your doubts be dispelled
Here's Dolly, she works in cosmetics
She curves like a cello as well

Dear Sirs, I'll not dilly with Dolly
She talks like she's swallowed some helium
Her IQ is akin to the duck
Other ducks all think of as really dumb

Dear Sir, so now you want intellect
Added to all that you seek?
Try Bertha the Bookworm whose hobby
Is tackling crosswords in Greek

(continued >)

Dear Sirs, I'll not bother Bertha
Who is bright in a very dull way
My partner needs to be funny sometimes
With wit, in love and in play

Dear Sir, if it's 'funny' you're after
You're in luck, she'll be along soon
Coco by name, a professional clown
She can make you a dog from balloons

Dear Sirs, but my partner must be
On occasion, a real class act
The picture of grace and refinement
(Which blowing up dogs, somehow, lacks)

Dear Sir, we've consulted our files
Taking note of all that you say
We found one, and one only, who matches
She'll be there by the end of today

Dear Sirs, I'm delighted! She's perfect!
Now a world-class romance has begun!
My thanks to you all at Life Inc.
For your help in this matter, well done!

Note to the reader: With a little imagination, you can adapt this poem to include almost any name. For example, the line, 'She'll be there by the end of today' can be changed to, 'Called Jane… so what do you say?'. This could make the poem suitable to send to someone you like.

Ship Of Stones

We walked on the hills by the coastline
We breathed the salt air of the sea
The ship of stones, it never changes
Or ages, unlike you and me

We knew then that somehow the light
Had gone from the love that we knew
We could tell, but chose to say nothing
Preferring the peace of the view

We studied the board full of facts
Slightly faded, not that we cared much
Took lunch in the tourist trap café
Chatted nicely, not one single touch

We drove home and found things to say
As the stars crept out on the black
Showered, politely agreed
We were tired, in bed, back to back

Our kiss at the station was awkward
As the cold razor light cut our ties
There was so much to say, or to try for
But all we could find was goodbye

I loved you like Satan loves sinners
Like dying men love a reprieve
For only your love let me find
Someone that I wanted to be

The ship of stones, it never changes
At the top of the hill by the sea
As I cry myself still for the knowing
That once there was you and me

Deadly

Of greed I really have no need
There's little that I crave
I'll gladly part with all I have
To go live in a cave

Wrath I simply can't pull off
I'm not a man of rages
To even go from calm to miffed
Can take me simply ages

To envy's little frenzies
I shall never much be prone
I couldn't give two hoots about
What others have or own

Gluttony will never be
My problematic issue
I'm fine with fresh air sandwiches
Washed down with morning dew

Sloth I surely will be loathe
To manifest or show
Morning noon and night with me
It's all 'Get up and go!'

Destructive pride I'll leave aside
I neither strut nor preen
Obscurity is fine by me
I've no need to be seen

For you, my love, I plan to live
In mostly virtuous splendour
But trust you must forever lust
For you's on my agenda!

Winters Child

First Winter

When you turned up at the party
I caught your eye by the stairs
For a moment the world disappeared
All that mattered was you being there
You were beautiful, simply beautiful
The one that I couldn't forget
My one and my only, I knew right away
Even though we'd only just met

Catching your love wasn't easy
We danced our steps pretty well
Little by little exchanging
Our feints of question and tell
When we got to the kiss... sweet fire!
That's when we knew we were lost
Our love was Saharan oasis
A bridge to forever we crossed

Second Winter

A year had passed, yet it seemed
Like every day was our first
Our love was defiant, relentless
No end to the joy or thirst
We were happily, madly entrusted
With magic we couldn't control
Held hands through all the illusions
Prayed to keep losing our souls

Our hearts were blind and devoted
As young hearts know how to be
The world was made for our laughter
The nights were made for our sleep
We hadn't a clue about anything
But we knew how to love and to hold
We were the greatest of alchemists
We could make time into gold

Third Winter

Now and again, I could tell
You thought things you didn't say
Sometimes I sounded impatient
Hated myself straight away
We argued a bit about money
We argued about the TV
Two people alone in a room
Who used to be you and me

We laughed, just not quite as often
We kissed, just not quite as much
Sensed an unsettling shift in the world
Felt it whenever we touched
We wanted to make it fresh again
We wanted to keep it the same
We tried every try worth trying
We agreed no one was to blame

Fourth Winter

You said you felt it was time.
We made love, then kissed goodbye
'Look after yourself', 'You too'
You brushed a tear from your eye

You were beautiful, simply beautiful
The one that I cannot forget
I know I have loved you forever
My one, my only, regret

Terms Of Endearment

A one-night stand
If ever one's planned
Involves little standing per se
A one-night stand
If memory be scanned
Is lying down, mostly, I'd say

Going out with you
Has little to do
With going out anywhere
Going out with you
To stick to the truth
Is mainly being in, and upstairs

Meeting for drinks
Is seldom, methinks
About wicked alcohol's curse
Meeting for drinks
Is your code for the kinks
That quench a quite different thirst

A nice early night
If I've got it right
Means not that fatigue has set in
A nice early night
Is your wording polite
For extensive intention to sin

One More

A trap for a fox or a furtive spy
Bricks in a wall built long and high
Wine on its side if it needs more time
The law down fast on a rascal's crime

Clues in a whodunnit book well-plotted
Tracks for a tram that it rides in, slotted
Cutlery for six when it's time for dinner
Bets on a horse that might be a winner

Stress on syllables sung in a song
Rumours to rest (assuming they're wrong)
A patio made for al fresco food
Secrets bare if you're in that mood

A cool beat down with a jazz drum kit
A wreath on Marilyn Monroe's crypt
Trails that lead to a secret nest
Some fields fallow when they need a rest

The blame for an act at someone's door
A carpet covering a shiny floor
Cables deep under restless oceans
Odds quite long on unlikely notions

Fears to rest so there's no more doubt
Your weapon down if peace breaks out
Low for a while if you're on the run
Towels on the sand under tropical sun

My dear, there are so many things you can lay
If you'd like one more…

                    …I'm free all day

Walnut Bread

It was a Tuesday when we got the news
You looked at me, but I hadn't a clue
What to do, and neither had you

We hugged, got teary, time stood still
You said, "It's the one thing I'm good at, being ill"
I said, "Well, don't forget singing off key"
You shrugged with a sniffle, simply had to agree

It looked like a pretty nice day for a walk
So we went outside, had a grown-up sort of talk
Including all the "It's so unfair!" stuff
That we had to, I guess, but a little's enough
We watched all the people, strolling about
Being unsympathetically normal, without
A care in the world, though you never can tell
Who is in heaven and who has a neighbour that's learning the accordion

You said let's make some walnut bread
So we stopped by the 'ARKET' (that's what the sign said)
Bought all the stuff, walked back up the hill
Got home and discovered another phone bill
Which I made into rather an excellent plane
(Well it wasn't in red so no need to pay)
Then into the kitchen for bread-making throes
You straight away dabbed some flour on my nose
Thus starting our All-Time Best Flour Fight
Ending with astronauts on Planet White
Then we calmed down a little, you Master me Slave
You told me to do things, I got in the way
But we got the job done, you and your pet oaf
Igor and Frankenstein: creating new loaf!

In the afternoon, we had sex
After, you talked about how you'd expect
Me not to want to be alone
That you understood I'd meet someone
To love, again, and that was okay
I had your blessing, but you hoped I'd wait
A little while, just a little while
To maybe think about you, and smile
As if you could doubt…
That's when all the words ran out
So I simply took your hands in mine
And we let the silence fill the time

During your foot rub, while 'Songbird' played
You went through some scrawly lists you'd made
Of things I had to promise to do
I said, "Well, I might, what's it worth to you?"
Then you threw a cushion and called me a twit
So I tickled you savagely, made you submit
Admit your feet were the stinkiest ever
And that *you* were the twit, while *I* was quite clever

Later, we made lots of crumbs in the bed
It really was excellent walnut bread
A tasty, wonderful, bedtime treat
(Not bad for a chef with stinky feet)

(*continued >*)

We talked a bit more, had a bit of a cry
Then you fell asleep in my arms and I tried
To sleep too, but I couldn't, so I started to pray
For the very first time and all I could say
Was, "Look, God, I'm sorry for doubting you
I just never felt all that stuff could be true
But if you are real and you felt you could spare
A small miracle now, well, then I swear
I'll do anything, truly, whatever you say
Just do your God thing, and allow her to stay"

Then I lay there, holding you close to my heart
Completely and utterly falling apart
Bitter and angry and sniffly and sick
You stirred and gave me a half-awake kiss
Saying, "Come on now, come on, don't be so sad
The walnut bread wasn't *that* bad"

Well, as it turns out, God's deaf or just cruel
So now, a year later, I still cry like a fool
At the simplest of things, and everyone's kind
I still play 'Songbird' a million times
Because you did, and I used to hate it so
But now it's a way to not let you go

The counsellor lady, she said I should try
Writing letters to you, but the pen doesn't write
Very well when the paper becomes rather damp
Besides which I checked and we're fresh out of stamps

I still don't forgive you, and I never will
Other guys have girlfriends who get a bit ill
It happens, you cope, take medicine and stuff
Then you recover 'cos otherwise love
Has to end. Well I don't agree, sorry, I don't
Never did, never will, don't want to and won't
Because I know *every* morning and *every* night
You were the one thing I ever got right
So I'll never forgive you for going away
And Tuesday is still a pretty bad day

Tonight I made some walnut bread
First solo attempt and let it be said
Perfection it wasn't, a bit dry I suppose
But I remembered to dab some flour on my nose

Get Thee To A Punnery

You said drop the puns, they're banal
So puns are now banished from sight
Henceforth, if you think that I use one
It's just a lick of the trite

- - -

I won't say your name means 'slut'
But I know last night on a whim
You went back home with a stranger
Then chose to sin on him

- - -

I see my intentions for us
Are now effectively toast
By this stage in the evening I hoped
That we'd be coital, post-

- - -

My love is like a red, red rose
So may I make my bid
To share with you my deoxyribo-
Nucleic acid?

Note to the reader: These are just four separate fragments of wordplay and are not intended to be regarded as a single poem. However, you can read them as a single item if you want to. You can see them as a vaguely coherent story of a troubled romance confounded by too much wordplay and other problems.

Not-With-You Days

Small stones on stained glass
That shatter and smash
Those spectacular sun-trapping visions
Rankly re-using their choreographed hues
In crystal-confetti derision
These are the not-with-you days

Slick swipes with a blade
Upon canvas and paint
That render a masterpiece ribbons
Thus scarring each stroke of the awe it invoked
In spits of insightless incision
These are the not-with-you-days

Raw stumps of defeat
Made of steel and concrete
Like scabs upon scented wild valleys
That jut their revile across gold-dappled skies
In wrecked angular cancerous malice
These are the not-with-you-days

The what-to-do, where-are-you
One-cup-of-tea-will-do
Wishing and fishing for clues about getting through
Angry at angriness, angrier nonetheless
Dreary old wearying
Not-a-two, not-with-you days

Magicians

You sweep aside the broken day
Lead me to the plotted scene
Of trespass new and terror play
Within your maze of woken dreams
To share the slow, rehearsed inception
Of your spectacular protection

Dissolving time, your hands provide
Your private healing, silent kiss
Savage bite, abrasive bliss
Upon my skin electrified
To taste the toxic incantations
Of your wicked, sly predation

You crack the battered, brittle frame
Of what I thought I knew of need
Teach my forcing pulse to crave
The blind and breathless pact's relief
We race to those far silhouettes
Where all the better worlds are kept

* * *

We are magicians of the sunrise
We are the wonder souls
This is the birth we realise
We dreamed but never told
Now we hold each other, in silent contemplation
While they name new constellations

A Considerate Lover

In that I love, I seek your finest self
In heart and mind content, and duly rested
Untroubled, calm, complete in vital health
No want of food or water ever tested
Right is this care, for if a frailness rake
The heart to which mine's linked, then so projects
That grievance into me, as does the lake
One bird of broken wing make twin reflect
Thus while expressing love, I seek, my dear
To still permit you fix hunger or thirst
Considerately choose one path sincere
To render love yet put your whole health first
Hence kiss I fullest deep your lips, yet think
To leave you free the while to eat or drink

Museums

Museums are where we make respectful pact
With former glories set in cases sealed
Preserve in airless rooms old artefacts
Their once great purpose now all but concealed
Guarded rooms allow partial display
Of parts and pieces meriting inspection
They educate, inspire and fascinate
Within a realm of stifling protection
These institutions are, beyond doubt, great
But yet, my dear, I pray you realise
It is a poor ambition to create
The same within the region of your thighs
Why stay locked in a past of dust becalmed
When there's a present for your private charms?

Candlelight

If you watch long enough, every candle
Gives up the fight in the end
Surrenders its light to the darkness
Runs out of fire to defend

That warm, proud, hypnotic brightness
Will falter, flicker then fade
Leaving behind only memories
Of a once magnificent flame

We can want, but we can't want forever
We don't work to eternity's scale
To persist, so they say, is a virtue
But not if you're sitting in jail

One glass of red wine for the memory
I watched as the wax grew cold
Thought of the song of your beautiful skin
The rhythms your eyes once told

One answer was all that I needed
From you, my incredible friend
But you chose just to watch as the candle
Gave up the fight in the end

Less Blind

Set by for me one chilling dawn
Of waking to a love that's calm
With kisses curtained, music playing by

Those private nights where you and I
Could let the darkness drift, and lie
While sharing truths
About this love of ours

Just set aside some pointless lines
Bad jokes that no one else could find
Slow footsteps as we reach the door
Turn a key but not before
You let me kiss you
Once again
Or maybe twenty times

Yes, keep such things as memories
Some letters, looks and what there is
In how we smiled
Kept each other near

Then going on to where you will
I ask you still
Don't give these things away
That made us close

For though a love can be less blind
Than lasting all of our lifetimes
A love that burns as bright as this
Admits of no last ever kiss

Labuan Bajo

In Labuan Bajo I watched the wild sun
Creating a furnace as vast as the sky
Spilling its riot of fires and gods
On a world made savage by what we deny

I spoke to the sunset in half-hearted whispers
Of hope I still harboured despite your last word
Watched as the bloodied and gold-speckled bay
Succumbed to the fade like a promise unheard

That's when I knew that all I had won
Were the splinters and driftwood of doubts I defied
Feeling the heat dissipate on my skin
I could let go, at last, of the last of the pride

From the ocean of predatory black silver crests
To the landscape of rusting and scorched amber flame
I lived every moment of tasting your lips
Then in the parched earth I scratched out your name

Swarming mosquitoes stood guard on the night
Riding the jasmine's sweet intoxications
The moon bled the colours and vanquished the heat
To the pulse of the tide's insistent invasions

So we search on and on, love always the prize
We steal from ourselves when we need it the most
In Labuan Bajo I watched as the sun
Took everything save one kiss from a ghost

Endgame

Your letter when it finally came
Was such a poorly framed endgame
All the moves so badly played
So this is how your beauty fades

Of course it's hard when looking back
To see your calculated track
That led to faith so well betrayed
By thrust and twist of jagged blade

The violence never could have won
If not for all the work you'd done
To be the new hope in my life
The closest and most trusted knife

To lay your heaven at my door
Teach my apprentice heart to soar
With every laugh, such pretty teeth
I never saw the skull beneath

You were a goddess worth the pray
I still acknowledge that today
I always will, I don't deny
Your greatness then, that place, that time

That's why I loved you, why I tried
To touch the healing sanctified
Despite a hundred warning signs
But who can warn the willing blind?

At least I had those precious days
Before you gave the game away
When trust and sweet belief could light
The fires to private paradise

So now you have apologised
Served up the meat beneath the flies
Offered up a second taste
Of cyanide in sugar paste

Sending me back down the years
To days and nights of acid tears
Of self-inflicted drunkenness
Hating more and loving less

Those times I sought the strength inside
To reach for easy sui-pride
Felt sickness raw in blood and bone
Demonic glyphs on heart of stone

Do I forgive? I do, of course
I did it long ago, remorse
Renews the scars upon the skin
I would not let you have that win

That said, if pressed for honesty
I know it cannot be complete
What you did's now a part of me
I can't escape your legacy

Sadder, wiser, yes, perhaps
The seasons turn, the memories lapse
I shrug, it was ten years ago
The ashen embers barely glow

But I did love you, loved you crazy
I want that written on the pages
I want the records to proclaim
At least I dared to touch the flame

I am not you, you are not me
That's all I need of victory
If still you must apologise
Just find a mirror...
                    and open your eyes

Told Off By The Lord of the Manor

Good Wench I've been given reports
Of the horses not getting their hay
So that, famished, they staged a small riot
Then kidnapped the Groom for three days

Good Wench some rumours I hear
You've not mown the lawns since the frost
Now the grass is grown taller than I am
With four of the gardeners still lost

Good Wench some news have I heard
Your sweeping the kitchen's quite poor
Leaving so many scraps for the mouses
Now some weigh five pounds or more

Good Wench I am told that last month
The cows were so often milked late
That in protest they dug a few tunnels
Thus (all but the fattest) escaped

Good Wench I am told it's so long
Since the ducks in the duck pond were fed
The ducks have now opened a bakery
As their best chance of getting some bread

(*continued* >)

Good Wench it has come to my ears
You've neglected to oil the clocks
So rust has crept into the workings
Now they tick when they're meant to go tock

Good Wench my sources inform me
You scarce ever collect the hens' eggs
So the hens, grown bored with the waiting
To pass time have all taken up chess

I've no choice but to give you a punishment!
At once to my chamber... undressed!
Should you keep on neglecting your duties
Quite frankly, I couldn't care less!

You Know The Way

You know the way that poets do
Exaggerate their love so true
With 'I'd do anything for you'
Mountains climbed and oceans blue
Traversed, apparently as proof
Of love that's passionate, undying
Line on line of rhyming, trying
To say 'I love you' in a way
Not used before in any letter
As if the striving wit's display
The crafty, stylish flick of phrase
Somehow makes it so much better?

That's really, truly, not my game
Could never be my trade or shame
But understand, this steady flame
Of light aimed at a single name
Just has to be conveyed or framed
In terms that will at least express
What little you may not have guessed
About my single hope and prayer
I need to give one honest view
In simple words of truth laid bare
Of simple love I want to share
You know, the way that poets do

Love's Knot

Love's not some words well-versed
Love's not lines on a page
Love's not lips sweetly-pursed
Love's not the heartbeats' rage

Love's not white roses' petals
Love's not melodic strain
Love's not diamond on metal
Love's not walks in the rain

Love's not signalled devotion
Love's not sly joyful tryst
Love's not taut-breathed emotion
Love's not long-lingered eyes

Love by these things is captured
As stars are by the lake
Counterfeit reflections
None but a fool mistakes

For love's not found in tokens
It lives in what's expressed
Through a life of somehow knowing
Of each, the other, 'Yes'

Signals

When will you start, my lovely friend
To heed the signals that I send?

I planted roses in the shape
Of your initials so they'd make
A nice display once fully bloomed
Did this not mean something to you?

Consider all those gifts galore
I bought for you (that's why I'm poor)
Silver, gold, fine jewellery
All of it etched 'With love from me'

Was it not clear enough, when I
Took several days to organise
Those fireworks, all synchronised
To blaze 'I love you' in the night?

Or what about the cake I made
The neat icing on top displayed
Your name inside a heart, my dear
Was not the message loud and clear?

I trained a parrot so he'd say
'Love you madly!' night and day
Gave him to you, perch and cage
Still my thoughts you didn't gauge

'Bride and wedding' magazine
I got you a subscription, keen
To see if you would get the clue
But no, still wasn't getting through

Did you really not suspect
That when I hired a string quartet
To serenade you at sunset
I hoped it would have some effect?

Recall the model Taj Mahal
From matchsticks, quarter life-size tall
I made in hope it would convey
My feelings in the clearest way

Or what about that billboard sign
Very tall, extremely wide
With your name and 'My love is true!'
You didn't start to get a clue?

I even felt it worth a try
Hiring a plane to cross the sky
Writing 'I love you' in white
Alas! Still no response in sight

Okay, so I exaggerate
But I have tried in my own way
To show how much you mean to me
But none so blind as you, it seems

When will you start, frustrating friend
To heed the signals that I send?

Upon Reflection

Placing honest thoughts in view
Is satisfying, through and through
Let it be said, romance with you
Is a state I would eschew

To never have you in my sight
I would declare a dream come true
To share a kiss by pale moonlight
Would leave me feeling sick and blue

To see the end of you forever
Sounds good to me without review
To spend another day together
My heart hopes that we never do

To lose touch 'til the end of time
Would bring me happiness on cue
Should you declare that you are mine
I'd feel regret is surely due

To watch you travel far away
I'd not resent or ever rue
To know you 'til I'm old and grey
I do hope not, it would be cruel

Shall you these words now misconstrue?

Shall you these words now misconstrue?
I do hope not, it would be cruel

To know you 'til I'm old and grey
I'd not resent or ever rue
To watch you travel far away
I'd feel regret is surely due

Should you declare that you are mine
Would bring me happiness on cue
To lose touch 'til the end of time
My heart hopes that we never do

To spend another day together
Sounds good to me without review
To see the end of you forever
Would leave me feeling sick and blue

To share a kiss by pale moonlight
I would declare a dream come true
To never have you in my sight
Is a state I would eschew

Let it be said, romance with you
Is satisfying, through and through

Placing honest thoughts in view

Naive In Vienna

We were happy on New Year's Eve
In Vienna, among all the crowds
A city-wide everywhere party
Dancing, romancing allowed
A million faces sugared in light
Vendors welcoming through-the-night trade
Crackers and fireworks tinting the sky
Smoke that hung as if never to fade

We were laughing on New Year's Eve
In Vienna, the city of cakes
Who knows how much Sacher Torte we had
Enough to be a mistake
The Hofburg was watchful magnificence
Shimmering bronze upon gold
Nothing but joy in our hearts
We were freezing — but were never cold

We were lovers on New Year's Eve
In Vienna, the jewel in the frost
We knew there was nothing but us
The old and the new, won and lost
Holding each other as dawn
Dared creep and discover the streets
The wreckage and flotsam of fun
That signalled transition complete

We shared New Year's Eve once
In Vienna, where time grows old
We whispered our love was forever
Intending that story be told
Saying goodbye to the city
I kissed you, then looked in your eyes
For the promise one day we'd return
To Vienna, where love never lies

Solophobia

No vertigo, I'm fine with heights
Don't mind even stormy flights
Confined spaces, cramped and small
Or open fields, I love them all

Don't fear reptiles, scaly snakes
Spiders don't give me the shakes
Creepy crawly weird insects
Not scared of any I've met yet

Technophobic? Not a chance
I love each new hi-tech advance
Being alone or lost in crowds
Neither leave me feeling cowed

The sight of blood is not a scare
I even like the dentist's chair
Jabs, injections, needles — these
I face with calm, unruffled ease

Poisons and toxicity
A common fear but not for me
Skulls, macabre ghostly signs
Send no shivers down my spine

I don't dwell on bad news or fate
Friday thirteenth is just a date
My one and only greatest fear?
That ever you might not be near

World Enough

Had we but world enough and time to take
The rubbish out in colour-coded ways
With everything recycled lest we break
The rules and bring about the end of days
Then glue that bit of broken tile and fix
Both pieces of the new TV remote
While patching up the sofa's newest rips
Before replying to that teacher's note
And fetch some bread — no, not that sort, the other
While choosing a nice card to send your mother

Then take the drooling dog to see the vet
Locate that old address book that we need
Install a filter on the internet
Adjust the thermostat as you decreed
Arrange the debits for the bills and check
No vital payments will this month be missed
Survey the wild debris, appalling wrecks
Of teenage bedrooms (call the exorcist)
And fetch some sugar — no, not that sort, the other
While choosing some fresh flowers to send your mother

Had we but world enough and time to mow
The lawn and fight the ever sprawling hedge
Replace the fuse that always seems to blow
Defrost the fridge, clean out the mouldy veg
Discover why the whatsit didn't record
Investigate the clunking boiler sound
Unravel seven slithering power cords
Switch off forgotten taps before we're drowned
And fetch some tea — no, not that sort, the other
While choosing gardening gloves to send your mother

(continued >)

Then list the shopping making careful note
Of stuff we have none of we'll need to buy
Then at the market mis-read what we wrote
So that, back home, we still have none — surprise!
Explore the storage cupboards, shelves and racks
To sling the stuff we don't need any more
Get nowhere fast, then put the whole lot back
It takes up twice the space it did before
And fetch some light bulbs — not that sort, the other
While choosing a warm scarf to send your mother

Had we but world enough and time to make
A soldier outfit (armour, sword and shield)
Help figure out the way verbs conjugate
Draw pretty pictures of magnetic fields
Then find our precious darling's purple socks
After finding where her shoes were hid
Step over roller skates and building blocks
While thinking back to when we *wanted* kids
And fetch some paint — no, not that sort, the other
While choosing ginger wine to send your mother

Then run an unpaid taxi service for
Karate, drama, football, swimming, chess
Gym, dancing, choir, cadets and flugelhorn
(Are we allowed to *discourage* interests?)
Be warden, healer, carrot, stick and lash
Detective, friend, drill-sergeant, kindly soul
The always open bank of easy cash
Pitchforking money down an endless hole
And fetch some poison, any sort will do
To feed your mother 'til she's stiff and blue

Had we but world enough and time for this
Perhaps we'd find one second for a kiss
The years fly by, you are still loved, desired
As I would show you, but... I'm *really* tired

Point Of View

Your looks, to be blunt, are not great
I doubt we'd make a good match
I'm stunning, of course (it's innate)
While you're much less of a catch

It's not just the face — the rest of you
Does not suggest 'brilliant lover'
I doubt that anytime soon
You'll be gracing a magazine cover

As for brains, I don't mean to cruel
But you're no intellectual star
I'd never suggest you're a fool
Except for those times when you are

You may think you're witty but I
Respectfully would disagree
Top marks for having a try
But I think I've seen funnier disease

Your friends are a motley selection
They do not impress me at all
I'd feel a much closer connection
If I talked to a solid brick wall

We've little in common, we spend
Our leisure in different ways
'I like you, but just as a friend'
Would seem the most relevant phrase

These lines maybe you will guess
Define a view not very keen
But please understand they express
Not what I see, but how I *am* seen

Having read *your* beautiful mind
To list all the problems you see
Please look in your diary and find
Some time to meet the real me

The cover is not the whole book
There's more to this story than 'No'
Let's meet, make time, take a look
You may find that, on you, I grow

Fantastabrill

A warm bath after a freezing walk
The perfect glide of a hungry hawk
A bus that comes just when you need it
A baby that burps each time you feed it
Impressive feats by acrobats
That great song at the end of 'Cats'
Your first kiss that included tongues
The days when you can do no wrong
The fascinating hues of coral
A piano delivered by Hardy and Laurel
The gleam you get from a shiny badge
A Shakespeare play that's really trag-
-ic, Jokes that no one else would get
Winning an unlikely bet
Though all these things are great, it's true
They're less fantastabrill than you

A slick beat kept by a good jazz man
An neat one-liner in a style deadpan
Sunset watched by a placid lake
Art snobs fooled by an amateur's fake
A jungle canopy rope bridge view
A secret only shared with you
The screams of kids on a rollercoaster
Thick-slice toast from a thick-slice toaster
Whodunnit tales with a neat plot twist
Catching up with a friend you've missed
Surf and sun with a Beach Boys song
When people say you were right all along
Ten minutes' play with a ten-week kitten
The second you know you're really smitten
Though all these things are great, it's true
They're less fantastabrill than you

An arrogant person treading on a rake
You drop something precious and it does *not* break
Zoos where you can feed giraffes
Stupid politicians' gaffes
Morning tea brought to your bed
Friends that like the books you've read
Harmony groups with perfect pitch
A scratch that gets right to the itch
Thoroughbred stallions pounding the flats
A cool guitarist in a silk cravat
The way that owls can spin their heads
The way that Ginger danced with Fred
The formula for adding up one to fifty
Judo moves that are slick and nifty
Though all these things are great, it's true
They're less fantastabrill than you

Back To The Rain

When the shadows flow back to your soul
When hope's scattered ashes are taking their toll
When the moonlight exposes the cracks
In every intention, defence and attack
I will hold you, my back to the rain
Of doubts that trap all of your angels in chains
Then kiss, in the silence, your hair
And stay 'til the world has learned to be fair

When the new's just as bad as the old
Destroying your faith in the shine you were sold
When your honest-to-goddess strong heart
Grows weary of ending up back at the start
I will shield you, my back to the rain
Of rage that could drive a saint far beyond sane
Then kiss, in the silence, your brow
And stay 'til the world has conceded new vows

When the maze doesn't have a way out
When you're left so unsure what the story's about
When you strive to be strong, without fears
As magnificent you wins a fresh set of tears
I'll protect you, my back to the rain
Of arrows with tips dipped in failure and pain
Then kiss, in the silence, your lips
And stay 'til the world, by this love, is eclipsed

Zelda's Song

Paint for me pictures of how you were then
A smile for all Time, a black and white lens
Erase the sad stories they tell in your name
Rekindle the fire with silver screen flame

Whisper to me about magazine covers
Your films and your songs, your secrets and lovers
One camera flash for each step off the plane
An elephant ride for Macy's Parade

Laugh again like that day on the beach
A flickering Super-8 smile beyond reach
"Is the blonde from a bottle?", "How goes it with Joe?"
But nobody asked where did the smile go

Show me the prints you crossed out in red
Tell me Chanel's all you wear when in bed
Sing to the soldiers or for JFK
Ignite all the rumours that burn to this day

Trace the ambitions that drove you so hard
Show me the letters that led to the scars
Dance through a century's Picture Post spreads
Laugh to hear Zelda called a Goddess

They say that the pain is the price of the fame
They say that the tears are part of the game
But I've seen your eyes in that faded old frame
I tell you the fame was the price of the pain

Let them ask how and let them ask why
Obsessed with farewells for a beautiful child
No answers now for the questions they ask
Zelda has learned to sleep, at last

Value

You were a very generous soul
Inclined to give me gifts galore
This seemed to be your chosen role
The queen of always giving more

You paid for this, you paid for that
Your credit card had friction burns
I could have been your spoiled brat
No silver pieces ever spurned

I could have learned to love the pain
Of purchase-predicated love
The circling of the silver chains
The sweetly snapped gold-plated cuffs

You sailed the straits of solvency
With cash for bait you got your fish
The hook went in so easily
Just gut and serve my every wish

Oh such a pity, Lady Lust
You gave so many things to me
But could not give me truth or trust
You could not give me honesty

You could not stop the fatal lies
The cancer in your dollar health
You could not make the truth a prize
Not for me, not for yourself

We could have found a different way
Could have been real, you and I
But forgery's your favourite play
And no one wants to kiss a lie

The last I heard, the world's the same
Love can't be bought at any price
You're sailing still, no chance of shame
Or ever being believed in twice

More Likely

Letters from Liszt to the King of Siam
Cast iron wings on a submarine tram
A soluble shoe
On a carpet of glue
In a house that's principally ham

Badgers with good astrophysics degrees
A rare kind of 5 that's half 93
An artichoke mill
On a musical hill
With matadors growing on trees

Feathers as heavy as bullion bricks
A bit of moss known for contortionist tricks
A functioning gill
On a pterodactyl
Who plays violin with a stick

Five dragonflies playing helical chess
An algebra based on 'Just have a guess'
A well-defined chin
On a skink full of gin
Plus a way to read this line that preserves the correct stress

Things I thought more likely to see
Than you ever sharing your love with me
It's nice sometimes to be wrong
So lusciously, hushes me, crushes me wrong

Autopsies written with topical jokes
An Elvis on Mars that isn't a hoax
Luminous soot
On a manatee's foot
In a sock that's earning to croak

One-ended hammocks with marzipan sides
Unicorn eggs, quite tasty when fried
Waterless Lochs
Where amphibious rocks
Do the tango with rigorous pride

Operas devoted to gardening tips
A Vegas casino without any chips
A map of the coast
That was bitten from toast
By a watering can with a zip

A way to put unicorn eggs in this line
That doesn't remind you about the last time
Icelandic monsoons
At Christmas in June
When Super Snails start to fight crime

Things I thought more likely to see
Than you ever sharing your love with me
It's a prize sometimes to be wrong
So lusciously, hushes me, crushes me wrong

White Light

I can see as many streets
As there are silent streets to walk
I can discuss, dissect the world
Until the world runs out of talk
I can see as many dawns
As my beating heart allows
Collect as many sorrows
As there are memories to plough

I can share the songs of laughter
Smiling eyes and wit provide
I can share the quiet sadness
Of those cut by jagged lies
I can tend as many wounds
As there are scars and hurts to heal
Touch the many reaching hands
Needing just a warmth that's real

I can fail as many times
As there are failings to defend
I can reach the paradise
Discovered in the trust of friends
I can brave as many storms
As there are droplets in the rain
Taste every dream or nightmare
Gifted to the sad or sane

Yet still when all is over
As remaining days grow fewer
I will feel nothing stronger
Nothing stranger, nothing truer
Than the love beyond all promise
That could only burn for you
White light you said you could not see
Or want, or ever choose

Rejoice

Though technically I'm morbidly obese no need to hate
I've joined a gym, in five years I'll be merely overweight
I've struggled to improve my drool (the world admires a striver)
These days when chatting there's much less conspicuous saliva

I can't deny I sweat a lot but recently I've showed a
Remarkable reduction in my distinctive body odour
My eczema's largely cured after many sad defeats, a
Special cream thrice daily makes my face less like a pizza

My triple-strength mouthwash now largely masks the halitosis
My head doctor has dealt with most of my deranged psychosis
With help my attitudes have gradually begun to soften
The voices in my head these days say 'Kill!' not quite so often

My therapist has fixed my awkward stutter and my lisp
It's only rarely now some thubtle thymptoms thtill perthitht
I've hardly any cold sores left thanks to the doc's endeavours
Though the discharge from my ears is sadly runnier than ever

The arson's over since I learned to build empathic bridges
I still think fire's pretty but I avoid the orphanages
It's true that the authorities maintain a file or two
But the dynamite's all gone and there is nothing they can prove

Having taking legal counsel I've cut all my former ties
With cults Satanic and attempted virgin sacrifice
My forehead 'HATE' tattoo I've had removed by using lasers
The scrotum 'DEVIL' one I'm going to leave I think for laters

This is my first attempt to write an ad for online dating
You lucky ladies can rejoice I'm single, here and waiting
Reply in haste I know this ad will leave you feeling cheered, though
Please include a photograph — I wouldn't want a weirdo

Lazy Lives

Ever browsed through books of verse
To find those 'just so' polished words
That capture what you want to say
With elegance? It takes all day
To find that nothing, so it seems
Is quite as good as it should be

A few come close, perhaps, but plenty
Are clumsy stabs at the elementary
Task of framing with good style
Your feelings. It is such a trial
You'd think that those
With talents in either verse or prose
Could find time in their lazy lives
To scribble something that's 'just right'
For you to copy out and send
To that most precious soul-mate friend
So you get credit for the finding
Practically the same as writing
Your own words, but if you went that way
What would the poets do all day?

Besides, the brilliant minds poetic
We're told have natural gifts aesthetic
To craft with rhythmic sense and taste
Some lines that can illuminate
The human condition or, if that's too hard
Be featured in cheap birthday cards

How nauseating, then, how sad
To search through books and find how bad
Most of them are at expressing your views
You get the feeling that their Muse
Sadly failed to set the seal
With artful wit on how you feel
That's how it seems, so no one looks
For very long through poetry books
Because they fail, both old and new
To say for me what I'd say to you

Knowing

Significance is sculptor
To the heart's unfired clay
Which none beyond its calling
May measure or assay

Give merchants all the gold
Give mariners the sea
Hand winners all their trophies
These all as naught to me

For I can walk beneath the stars'
Silenced eternal silvered shine
Then think a while on you
And know the world be mine

Needs

I need the remarkable calm of your touch
That banishes cares and scares and such
The infinite solace I taste as you reach
To kiss me, and all of the lessons you teach
With your eyes

I need mornings when, saturated with sleep
We draw close, cheek to languorous cheek
The after-sex, after-dream slumber we share
My fingers exploring your dishevelled hair
Like a prize

I need distant vacations, beaches and caves
Castles and ruins, hot touristy days
Suitcases, travel guides, tickets and passes
Passports unfindable, sat-on sunglasses
That photograph well

I need candlelit dinners, the soft focus trance
Of a love that can play with the clay of romance
Orchids and whispers, waltzes so gracious
Lady and Gentleman, glances flirtatious
As hell

I need things that go wrong, intentions that sink
Without trace, lost keys, toothache, spilled ink
So it's your turn or mine to be solver and fixer
Hero and healer, great Jungian trickster
With know-how for two

I need pillow talk, our genius drivel
Tea-for-two parties, jokes that we giggle
About for years, though we can't recall now
What started it off, or when, who or how
But I bet it was you

I need the ash days of still, silent rooms
When sadness creates a 'Why bother?' cocoon
With much to be said, but the saying would fail
So we reach, hands sharing their comforting braille
As light fades

I need that unmerciful play in your eyes
When you're way ahead of me, stealthy and sly
Of course then I fall — smack! — into your trap
While you watch, self-amused, privately happ-
-Y in spades

I need the text messages, brazen, obscene
About things they don't show on a cinema screen
The sweat, the exhaustion, the passion, the heat
The endless creative disruption of sheets
We adore

I need the gray hours of day-to-day stuff
Chasing the pennies, we do what we must
Not a high, not a low, no joy, no dread
But at least in the end we can flop into bed
Kiss. Snore.

Exploring together, in life and in love
What it means to be here, to be now, to be us
Grant me this, and in truth, I have no other needs
For us is the best of all things I could be

Good Mourning

Walk-sleeping, I scythe up my mail
Dawn's harvest of junk and bad luck
Five bills all demanding attention
I feel like a parenting duck

The man who is just a waist upwards
His grin on its autocue tether
Has links to live places where things have gone wrong
Plus plausible fibs about weather

In the shower the water's just perfect
Alternately freezing and Hades
One blob of shampoo in my eyes and I look
Like a zombie bush baby with rabies

My tea is much darker than wanted
Since the servants forgot to get milk
I sip, and I gaze at the table
A riotous Rorschach of spills

Whoever it was designed morning
Has left little scope for kind praise
It's the hippo of diurnal phases
The Edsel of times of the day

Harsh judgement, I know, but deserved
As I flinch at the sky's grizzled hue
For this, I rose from my slumbers?
For this, I stopped dreaming of you?

A Richer Faith

From time to time the story forms before my eyes
Each sound intrigues as do the shifting scenes
Discovered tales unfurl and slyly tantalise
Entwining what could be with what has been

These visions are a richer faith's reality
Not merely puppets of my magic mind
I will not slander them as merely fantasy
The love must see before the heart can find

I see, towards the end of May, a lazy sky
The sun descending, proud but not too strong
Creating worlds of summer scents and shaded sighs
I wait and call to mind one special song

Just by Palazzo Madama's radiant face
The ancient and the new in one combined
We meet, we hug, you smile and straight away you race
Through wishes locked and loved within my mind

You share your privileged take on life's dull treachery
This careless, unfair world's survival trials
The sweet infusion of your voice seduces me
Again, I sympathise with rueful smiles

We find a place just by the square to sit and eat
I try to not get lost within the trance
You order for us both while I politely cheat
Steal yet another saved forever glance

As time moves on I judge when I should take the reins
To lift you, make you laugh, bring back the light
Restore the sworn alliance of the broken chains
Help conjure up the you that wins the fights

A touch of retail therapy is clearly due
Vast Via Garibaldi calls your name!
The kingdom of the credit card has summoned you
We rush towards the shrines of fashion's flame

You browse and choose and look, refuse and change your mind
Assess each cut and fabric, line and hue
Relentlessly you sift and search and swoop to find
The special gems created just for you

You ask me what I think about the shape and fit
This does, of course, require a lingering stare
A glorious excuse, I make the most of it
Well, after all, my verdict must be fair

It's clear that every angle has to be assessed
You pose and turn, I study all the facts
Your every curve commands my keenest interest
I mentally indulge in various acts

I give my views, you make a choice, we go to pay
A trick of plastic and the magic's done
Outside the sun's descent declares the end of day
As evening's rituals are just begun

We make our way south-east across the city streets
Of course we find Vittorio Veneto
We find a café, sit outside where we can see
Chiesa della Gran Madre di Dio

The air is warm with just a barely noticed breeze
The tourists swarm, the bars do roaring trade
Your mood is brighter now, we play, we laugh and tease
My love each time you smile at once remade

(*continued >*)

We pause, and as the silence fills the fading light
Your eyes whisper their secret into mine
You let me know this is the place, this is the night
When placid water shall become new wine

I walk you to the bridge, just where the steps descend
Towards the bustling riverside cafés
I look at you, for years the finest of all friends
We know there is no more we need to say

We hold each other close in good conspiracy
We close our eyes and kiss
There is no time, there is no space, no you or me
There is no world or anything but this

The story knows its way towards the morning sun
No need to paint those private, sharing hours
The ancient city witnesses new love begun
It has its secrets and stands guard on ours

From time to time the story forms before my eyes
This is a richer faith's reality
Discovered tales unfurl and slyly tantalise
With where you are, and where you ought to be

Twisting

Love is a twisting
Of sparks pre-existing
That arc on the kindling
Of kinder intent

Love is a questing
For tones of attesting
That sonar the fathoms
Of favour's consent

Love is a misting
Of lines of resisting
That sign the surcease
Of soloist station

Love is a healing
A scar-less redeeming
That harnesses hope to
The heart's aspiration

Positive Thinking

I never thought I stood a chance
Because with every stolen glance
I felt you were too good for me
Tens don't date a two or three
But people say stay positive
Pursue your dreams and dare to live
Feelings should not be denied
How will you know if you don't try?

A friend said how he heard before
That men will often just ignore
The gorgeous girls, since they assume
There is no chance for love to bloom
Which leaves the girls feeling rejected
Sad, alone, their looks neglected
Because guys shrug and think "No way!"
Give up and simply stay away

"Well, not *this* guy!", I said to me
I'll go about things differently
Be bold and strong and resolute
Be undeterred and give pursuit
Choose the moment, ask you out
No trace of hesitance or doubt
Thus gallantly alleviating
Your sad and lonely days of waiting

That's why I went right up to you
Looking like you always do
Beguiling, lovely, sweet perfection
Nature's beautiful reflection
Angel, princess, hot, divine
Stunning as the stars that shine
A face to love at any cost
And what you said was, "Get lost"

So… right the first time
Well done me
Still got the gift of prophecy!

I think I'll make a cup of tea
What's on TV?

Independency

In the prime of his life, the peak of his powers
The height of his talents and skills
Resolute, independent, quite his own man
Accomplished, successful, fulfilled

Known for his confidence, judgment to match
Fair strong in body and mind
Nobody's fool and nobody's slave
With the courage to speak as he finds

The life and the soul, the salt of the earth
Determined, with plenty of drive
A good man to have in your corner
A tough customer when it's required

It's all there on the record, no pushover he
Give that man in the mirror his due
So why does he find a small tear in his eye
If the phone rings and it isn't you?

Half A New Day

Half a new day plus half an old night
The tale of the fail as stale as the wine
I'd settle for this, if only the light
Could brighten my heart, obscene of the crime

Taken for granted, or granted all takes
Tides of re-think and wisdom by sleight
Pointless of course, but I'm glad of the fakes
The counterfeit craft of weathered hindsight

Half an old night and half a new day
Seeing hope try to take flight in thin air
Silence too loud for the nothings to say
Much greater than one, much less than a pair

So here's to all that, that led to all this
A banquet of leftovers, cold tea and scraps
As I pick up the peaces and gently air-kiss
Your pitcher plant lips, the prettiest of traps

Addiction

Against my wish the drug invades
Degrades my ruddied skin and slips
Its savage grip into my blood
I taste the flood of toxic trip
As my unfit, unsettled heart
Starts to race against the fix
Yet thereby greater fires the mix
Such is the sick and stealthy trick
Of this unfortunate addiction

My eyes should both be locked away
Detained for their so deadly trade
To let you just invade my stare
Snare me with the views they made
My gaze degraded by this fuel
So cruel of raw injected vision
Pure and deadly light incision
That fixed me in the heaven prison
Of this unfortunate addiction

You ought to be arrested too
So compelling, glacial cool
To rule me, make me contemplate
My surest fate, dependent fool
I race, make haste, to try to trap
Lock snap the time, freeze the craze
Fossilise light's biting rays
Then figure out the mauling maze
Of this unfortunate addiction

The deed is done, the web is spun
What fun for you to play, seduce
Constrict the noose, make me crave
Another wave of lust abuse
No rest or truce from this deft curse
The raging thirst that you inflict
Dependency that none has kicked
One glance confines me to the crypt
Of this unfortunate addiction

All Of This

The deepest rhythm of faith I've known
The dawn that cracks the sameness drone
Fugues of foolishness in touches
Burning all my failure's crutches
Gravitation's dance that binds
Our best determination's find
The arrow that can never miss
I find our love is all of this

Cheetah runs of flexing lust
Petra citadels of trust
Worlds in grains of knowing glances
Rigged roulettes of locked-in chances
Devotion sure as time's direction
Certain as a liar's defection
Seductive and slow-motion bliss
I find our love is all of this

Fears hunted, staked, cremated
Give and take uncalculated
Glory like Mojave eagles
Familiarity like sequels
Healing for regret's disease
The chain that only ever frees
Nectar sparks of stolen kiss
I find our love is all of this

Trance amid desiring's flak
Symphonic wants that fade to black
Pleasured eyes no longer blind
Skin on fire from melded minds
A psychic chemistry of needs
With psalms from co-created creeds
A two-heart 'can do' genesis
I find our love is all of this

Feelings

Each sense I own, for being denied love's fire
Is now cast into shade of sadder guise
For what feeds one, feeds not the soul entire
Slakes single need, but leaves the rest unprized
Your images, beguiling to my sight
My arms resent for being beyond caress
While softly-spoken words in still of night
Delight mine ear, but coax the eyes' distress
Thus have your lips, which wait for me conjoined
Likewise paired here both joy and its converse
Have love and love's denial so alloyed
As gold with ashes, light and light's reverse
No fix but one's within this servant heart:
To come to you, and then, thy lips to part

Restriction

The painter given but one single shade
Would find his inspiration cruelly choked
Likewise the tunesmith would reject his trade
If made to grace the stave with just one note
The chef confined to one ingredient
Would likely fail prepare a fine repast
So too the dancer's muse would soon be spent
If forced to use one step from first to last.
Thus how am I new verse to give express
When all you give is love, in thought and deed?
Love refined, love good and love endless
Invariant, so strong and fierce and sweet?
Since purer be the source, the less may be distilled
Love serves least well the verse that best a life fulfils

Looking For You

I looked for you among my friends
As well as friends' friends too
Checked all the dating agencies
They didn't have a clue
I looked at profiles, set up dates
A swamp of 'when and where's
Looked high and low but still no show
You've made yourself quite scarce

I went to singles parties, mingled
Few have mingled more
Mingled madly, gladly, got the
'Best Mingling' award
I was the bon viveur
The life and soul, the socialite
I partied, flirted, searched and hurted
Still no you in sight

I travelled, trekked and searched the world
To find your lovely face
From Kaffeklubben Island
To Antarctica's chill wastes
Sailed the seas to reach Attu
Climbed trees on Vanua Levu
Grazed my knees and caught the flu
Couldn't catch a trace of you

I asked a psychic known to be
Among the best, the purist
She did the voodoo few can do
But couldn't guess where you is
Then I turned to science, NASA
Let me use the Hubble
I scanned the universe but found
Just starry dust and rubble

Okay, you win the hide and seek
I'm out, I'm done, I quit
Finding you I think I've proved
Is quite beyond my wits
I had a look most everywhere
East, west, below, above
Perhaps now you could just reveal
Where do you hide, true love?

Punting

When I paid you a visit in Oxford
You said, for something to do
Let's take a punt down the river
It's fun for an hour or two

By that stage wholly besotted
I would have said yes to whatever
I wanted so much to impress you
So it seemed like a fitting endeavour

You were gorgeous and sexy and lovely
Relaxed and reclined in the punt
Quite the romantic scenario
I maintained a dignified front

The Cherwell was calm and serene
My gondolier act wasn't strained
Plenty of smiling and laughter
It was going so well. Then it rained.

Rained?

Like a Biblical flood re-enactment
Like hell with water for fire
Like a form of soggy entrapment
Like a storm of infinite ire
Like a symphonic ode to rain water
Like the clouds went back for refills
Like we'd upset Poseidon's daughter
Like evolving back towards gills
Like Morse code sent via thunder claps
Like getting a raindrop tattoo
Like an Armageddon of drippy taps
Like life inside a flushed loo
Like a fire extinguisher artillery
Like a stabbing with watery arrows
Like a pummelling water-based pillory
Like a thrash in a pool without shallows
Like the sky was a vast soda siphon
Like a canyon becoming a lake
Like a planet rain tried to grow life on
Like an ocean given a shake
Like we were the magnets of moist
Like rain clouds having a rant
Like death by drowning rejoiced
Like a garden hose killing ants

(continued >)

With all the rain, as you'd expect
We ended up just a little bit wet

Wet?

As wet as an otter's origami
As wet as an iceberg's underside
As wet as a city, post-tsunami
As wet as a used teapot's inside
As wet as a deep-sea diver's saliva
A wet as paint that's just gone on
As wet as a white shark's conjunctiva
As wet as when the wet's no fun
As wet as a surfing champion's vest
As wet as a big blue whale's spittoon
As wet as a homing mermaid's chest
As wet as seas aren't on the moon
As wet as a dipsomaniac's throat
As wet as a Cornish coast breakwater
As wet as life lived in a moat
As wet as a lemming's rush to slaughter
As wet as a frisky frogs webbed bits
As wet as poor Titanic's anchor
As wet as Aquaman's armpits
As wet as whatever than dank is danker
As wet as an arctic trawler's nets
As wet as a pelican's diving plunge
As wet as a water playground's jets
As wet as a ship that's made of sponge

We survived, somehow, and retreated
To your room from that watery feud
Of course we needed to change
So removal of clothing ensued

Then, to my delight, things progressed
In a happy and natural way
One thing led to another (and another, and another)
Nobody saw us for days

When I paid you a visit in Oxford
We were blessed by that weathery quirk
The happiest time of my student life
I guess praying for rain really works

Her Morning Phone Call

Let the hummingbirds learn to be humless
Then take all the buzz from the bees
Unplug every rock'n'roll band in the land
Make it strictly illegal to sneeze

Put soap on the bows of violinists
Slap rubber on every church bell
Convince opera singers to chew upon glue
While muzzling parrots as well

Dismantle all known karaoke machines
Take a hammer to all the jukeboxes
Let talk show presenters hop off a cliff top
So they plunge down to where all the rocks is

Switch off all the engines of aircraft
They make such an infernal racket
Let all the small crickets and chirruping things
Be muffled in tiny straitjackets

Take people who slurp at their tea
Somewhere dark to be strangled quite quick
Put all of the buskers who croon out of tune
In a sack, in a lake, with a brick

As for traffic, let all the cars halt
So a stillness descends on the roads
Say the right of all frogs to croak is revoked
With an equal restriction on toads

Tell the dentists to switch off their drills
Make tap-dancers dance in their socks
Put an end to the rustling breeze in the trees
While evicting all cuckoos from clocks

Let the street-corner preachers use semaphore
Let politicians all be struck mute
Suggest to the sheep that it's neat to not bleat
Tell the owls it's astute to not hoot

Let the stadium crowds remain hushed
They can show their support in sign language
Let the sloth be considered the fellow to follow:
Silent and placid and languid

For all noise is a witless distraction
Undeserving the air that we breathe
There is only one sound worth the hearing:
The words of my lover to me

Transformations

I have seen fresh snow transform as it lies
Into a slurry of nothingness gray
A log fire's flickering vaudeville of sighs
Grow cold as confession, black as the grave
I've heard songs, musical rapids of dance
Become noise, jagged rips in the fabric of sound
As wine's dark blood of hinted romance
Dissolves, becomes water, sorrows undrowned

The crimson and gold of the sun's steady rise
I have seen become drizzle and featureless cloud
Observed streets fill with your face and your eyes
To jeer at my solitude lost in the crowds
I have witnessed our bed of hungers nocturnal
Become a dark maze of cactus and blade
Where most precious cares, nurtured or learned, all
Flake into phantoms that mock as they fade

All this when you hide so far beyond reach
When you lock away all of the love that you teach
Sealed in the hurting, wrapped in the dark
Stripped to the silence of your troubled heart

Reach

Far from the graze of the fables I told
To my younger heart's ill-advised panning for gold
Far from the towering silos of lies
Wherein we store all of our favourite sighs

Far from all this, you walk and you teach
Far beyond anything beauty could reach
You whisper your heresy into my sleep
Conjure confusions about what could be

You trick the perspective, you lecture the class
You crack all the mad metaphorical glass
That usually gets in the way of these crimes
Of discovery, the glittering 'maybe' times

So having no luck in ignoring your voice
Reluctantly drawn to the lava of choice
Aware that the hourglass rations the sand
I know that it's time, and reach for your hand

Piazza San Carlo

The ghost of Piazza San Carlo
She dances her trance towards me
Draws in the air all the pictures
She could not allow me to see

She would smile if not for the sadness
She feels for all lovers denied
Then warns me of love and the burning
That comes from the echoes of 'Why?'

As she speaks, her voice has the fire
Of innocence lost to the rust
Saying she could reveal anything
Except for the things that she must

On her hand is the stripe of the blood
From the cut of her need to be free
Washed in the wine of the love
That we understood never could be

As real as the best of mythologies
Her voice still takes to the air
Eternal, etched deep in the stones
Of the sun-bleached facades of the square

I scream at her still, and protest
With a pounding and bloodied heart's rage
At the madness we made of our chances
Blank spaces we left on the page

The ghost of Piazza San Carlo
She dances her trance towards me
Lost to the dreams and denials
Of a love that was never believed

Prayers

I don't pray to gods the most
I pray instead to chat show hosts
Because if they would see this book
Take an interest, take a look
Then interview me, that can't fail
To give a little boost to sales

Although I pray to chat show hosts
I also pray to all of those
Brilliant people, minds so keen
Who work on papers, magazines
Because if they would write about
This book that too would help, no doubt

The point being that if I can make
A bit of money, I can take
You to see the isle of Kuta
(There is no destination cuter)
A beautiful, impressive place
Romantic too? Well, just a trace

If we went there, I cannot say
What would happen, how the play
Would then unfold but I suspect
We'd get on well, perhaps select
Romance, in all its loving fun
Kisses lit by setting sun

So media people, I love you all
Listen to the prayers that call
To you, from Mr. Unknown here
A little plug, a little cheer
Could help to make this dream come true
Besides, you know, I'd do it for you

Friends And Lovers

You say I should not eulogise
Yet you possess a sweet sunrise
To other hearts all locked, denied
Which once you shared, with touch and smile

I know, I know, the feelings change
So friends and lovers trade their names
While sharing special kinds of pain
With every loss, each one a gain

But never ask me to forget
The heartbeats that, as you once slept
I felt to touch your hair, your neck
To look upon you, and protect

Or all the times I felt one fear
That ever you might not be near
Shed, as well, one bitter tear
You could take so long to appear

So now, to this, the turning page
To love you as a friend, you say
Which one request with me remains
The easiest promise ever made

Provided this, that you will know
Deep as your heart's unfaded glow
The sun may set, the warmth remains
Not all of love is as love named

Ommadawn Girl

First, there were not any kisses
For reasons she knew, as did I
Something to do with the stars
Not being very neatly aligned

I waited, she said I was patient
The waiting went on for a while
I made her a heart — origami
Was one way of passing the time

Then Halloween came, in the darkness
She uncovered her story and score
Took off the masks with a shrug
Said nothing can hurt any more

She decided to play Ommadawn
I made hot chocolate for two
She rested her head on my shoulder
Then we kissed, nothing better to do

Through the night, we talked about everything
Put all the scars on display
Shared a few relics preserved
From epics of love's fickle ways

By sunrise we'd made the new pact
Let's love, we said, but not fall
We were tired, of course, hadn't slept
One kiss became yawns, I recall

We were great, for a time, as survivors
Sharing the joy of new trust
Flying too close to the sun
Of course, as all lovers must

There was mystery, madness, affection
Ice-cream, sulks and repairs
All of the glitter and litter
That comes with a lover's leap dare

In the end, my love wasn't quite
Enough to slay demons and pride
Perhaps we most loved one another
When we came to the end of our ride

Always, she'll be my Ommadawn girl
The music plays on, every theme
Is a kiss to the air, to the memory
Of love that was never a dream

Café Thingy

I remember the pavements on Charing Cross Road
Wannabe diamonds in flak attack rain
The lamps divulging their auras of gold
On scuttling figures just missing their trains

September, the month when summer caves in
Had served up her riot of fun-ending tricks
It was cold, wet and late, we were fish without fins
We craved an indoors and caffeine-ish fix

Down by the station, we found the Café
It had the greatest of virtues: open
One in the morning, two rather damp strays
With guesses suspected but never yet spoken

We were the solitary waifs in the place
Just windows between us and death by monsoon
London was wearing her fall-asleep face
Drizzle and weariness, one-quarter moon

You stirred cappuccino, I sipped at my tea
Surrounded by posters from long-ago plays
In subtle stage whispers we came to agree
Some of the pictures had seen better days
("Like I have", I said — I'm witty that way)

You were the visitor, I was the host
This was my city, a circus of drains
You were enchanting, my hopes were all toast
The tablecloth featured some interesting stains

I was trying so hard to guess the next moves
Unsure what you wanted, or needed to be
Goddess in blonde, eyes without clues
Funny as hell, and yet... there with me

(continued >)

The rest of the city was just a blurred view
None of it mattered, all I could feel
Was the singular oddness of being there with you
While nothing outside was important or real

You were secrets in puzzles, enigmas in twists
You were fantasy chance-to-be, answers unasked
You were beautiful, brilliant, none could resist
But I knew there were reasons for such a bright mask

After two hours, failure and I
Made our peace, once again, as old friends often do
I pretended to notice the time, all surprised
Brilliant acting you may have seen through

But then, without warning, you said the four words
Time froze, I was stunned, transfixed by the spell
I went blank, it felt so surreal, absurd
I'm glad that I handled it so very well

You smiled, you were kind, I think that you sensed
I was hypnotised, trapped in the joy of no choice
But you didn't know, never could, all that it meant
To hear those words from your beautiful voice

I shall never forget Café Thingy or how
Four words re-wrote the whole story of me
Led to a journey that, looking back now
I know was the best of the worst I can be

So long, long ago, where are you today?
I hope that sometimes you remember it too
The rain and the night when, in a Café
We found a new world, the way lovers do

Unwritten

This is the poem unwritten
About the love not loved
The wanting never wanted
For not being good enough
This is the memoir traced
Across the barren, desert page
The passion unignited
Giving way to unheard rage
This is the tear unnoticed
On the diary never read
The wishes that, all left unwished
Leave nothing to be said
This is the unfelt silence
Of the never shared embrace
That will always, always haunt me
When I look upon your face
In the photograph I took
The only one I still possess
That answers every question
With all I have… a guess

Vacation

Come stuff my face with cheesecake, damsel fair
Enjoy foot rubs and tea the evening long
Go to The Magic Castle, deign to share
Flawed strum of mis-remembered smoochy song!

Come pillow fight with me, then let us share
Rude plans in showers, post-nocturnal sport
View movies with a Zinfandel quite rare
Or visit jazz clubs of a tuneless sort!

Gaze from a mountain view when sun's descended
Then pounce on me with kiss and frisky tongue
Make overtures that go far beyond friendly
Exhaust me in ways Puritans think wrong

Walk Venice Beach attired as men do dream
Enjoy fair Coronado's twilight views
Then lead me to your bed for deeds obscene
Or just that I may read aloud to you

Do with me as you wish, just let this paradise persist!
My ticket home's ripped in the trash… it never will be missed!

Hotel Bel-Air

If I could now go anywhere
I think I'd choose Hotel Bel-Air
Stone Canyon Road's own heaven made
For all the games of love we played

I often think about the day
We found each other, made our way
You trapped me with your mischief eyes
I could not answer or defy

The dining room's neat calm perfection
Fed our love with sweet confection
Arm in arm we walked the grounds
Still unsure of what we'd found

That night we knew the world was ours
Among the subtly backlit flowers
Of course we stopped to kiss, alone
The sweetest secret ever known

So many years, they go so fast
Yet still sometimes I touch the past
With you, whose love, gold heart, sweet care
I knew once in Hotel Bel-Air

Confection Of Chains

Our scrapbook of chances, declined or unspoken
Our story of promises, stolen or broken
All wrapped now, bandaged, sarcophagus dry
In the lock, never prized, of the memory's eye
My heart, if it could, would scream to deny
This chapter was never much more than a token
Of what could have been, or could have been tried

Our rituals physical, infatuated
Our nocturne of whispers, wilfully fated
Are sullied now, slandered by silent response
By faraway looks, your choice to be one
Yet I would, if I could, rip the mask from the con
Rekindle the laughter that cost what you hated
To share the completion of what had begun

Our prison of fears, confection of chains
Our preference infernal for scars to remain
Combined in their puppetry, walked us through fires
Bloodied wrists pierced by doubt's silver wires
We wanted to heal but could not conspire
To coax what we shared into salve for the pain
Nothing left but a photo, the kiss of the liars
To tell of my love that never flew higher

Declaration of Interest

In a perfect world with a perfect me
With a perfect you (which you seem to be)
I'd tell you all this face to face
Judge the perfect time and place
I'd be my cool and confident best
I'd be impressive, you'd be impressed

You'd listen to my charming phrases
Laugh, confess you'd hoped for ages
I would make a move some day
Then hold to me in a smoochy way
Off we'd go, all smile and kiss
Arm in arm, romantic bliss
Soft focus sunset, rousing theme
Just like a classic movie scene

But that's more easily said than done
Believe me failing is no fun
I have tried, really, lots of times
Never, ever get it right
I talk to you in a chatty, self-conscious, rambling way
Idly pass the time of day
Bit of a laugh, not-very-good joke
Then I think "Say it now!", but of course I choke
Never express what I really intend
So then the chat just sort of… ends
Pleasant smiles, you walk away
I win Biggest Loser again, hurray!

I really like you, that's the truth
Because, well… I simply do
A bit more than just as a friend
In fact a lot more, but I'll bend
The facts for now, don't want to scare you
(Or myself, I wouldn't dare to)

The thing is, as you may have guessed
When it come to words, I'm not the best
So I got this from a book done by
Some unknown Rowland something guy
It's all love lines, romantic verse
Nothing great (though I've seen worse)
To be honest not my kind of stuff
But I looked for one verse good enough
To copy and send, to you from me
Which now I've done, obviously

I don't know what you'll think or feel
About this clumsy crass reveal
Of all my secret inner thoughts
I could not easily say before
(Well, I still haven't *said* them, technically
But this is 'as good as', I hope you'll agree)

You're great, a star, you really are
I have enjoyed being friends so far
But I feel I'd like to be lots more
So perhaps you'll let me know the score?

A really, excellent way to do this
Would be with a long, deep smackeroo kiss
Plus the bit where you insist on a wild, crazed, debauched,
                                  frenzied, ravishing night
Or we could have some tea if you like
A movie? Whatever, I really don't care
So long as you and I are there

Before you rush to say, "No chance!"
Reject this so-high-class advance
Just let me say…

(*continued* >)

It wouldn't hurt to give me a break
I'm neither failure nor a fake
I've lots to give, I'm always clean
It could be fun (or at least obscene)
I'm worth a shot, a try, a dare
Worth at least a pizza shared
Okay, I'm nice, but not too much
I really can do raging lust
I know that's something you might doubt
But I can… er, TMI for now?

So I've been brave and sent you this
I guess by now you've got the gist
I will not beg, I've got my pride
Though *please say yes or else I'll die*
(That was a joke — I'm quite okay
I'm not a psycho) (not yet anyway)

But if you do say yes I'll try
To love you morning, noon and night
In a perfect world, or as near can be
With a perfect you (which you are to me)

Vegas

What goes on in Vegas
Stays in Vegas
That's what she said to me
That's why this page is
The shortest, vaguest
Probably laziest
Poem that you'll ever see

Perception

Change how you look and you change what you see
What shall you choose when you look at me?
Companion, friend, lover to watch over you
Season by season, by sun and by moon?
Or a song played once in the gilt of the night
Before the raw chill of morning's new light?
Mine not the choice, mine not the decree
But I'll reach out to you if you reach out to me
Change how you look and you change who you see

A Day At The Zoo

Another of your rotten ideas
It was windy and rainy all day
You were in a foul mood — big surprise!
Most of it was shut anyway
I lost my wallet somewhere
One of those turtles was dead
To be honest, the best bit was the Mars bar
We should have stayed home instead
Me and you
La di dah di dah
A day at the zoo

117

X Rated

Deceiving in style
The camouflaged guile
Of your quite sudden feeling
This 'we' thing's a trial
Is impressive enough
Though the scars cut up rough
When I think of the needing
The joyous re-seeding
Of hope, love and healing
We managed, quite well, for a while

It's not really stealing
Your come and go feelings
Are just one more trust
I now won't be needing
This time I can hope
That I know how to cope
Like a proud loser must
As the miscreant lust
Becomes dry, settled dust
That obstructs each chance of believing

What rhymes with 'redeem'?
Very little, it seems
Not us, anyway
So much for this team
We had so much to give
But it gave, so we live
With the mystery play
Of the words we can't say
As the silences slay
The feelings we shared in a dream

So we cut to the scene
Where the words never mean
What we really intend
Just gripe the slate clean
But I do mind the kill
Of this love, that is still
And the way you defend
A choice love cannot mend
Because I can't pretend
Not to know what we could have been

Winter Stale

December's useless invention
Of static solstitial despair
The charmless lack of convection
Frost's skeletal grip on the air
Conspire to lock my intentions
In a casket of less, couldn't care

The woods, by minimalist pen
Made black graffiti on plate
Each bird a master of zen
Resigned to his feathery fate
Waiting an hour or ten
For something on which to predate

Mud transmuted to metal
Skies of wet flannel sheets
Slush invading to settle
In the socks in the shoes on my feet
As I race to the shrine of the kettle
A loser of every heat

The seasonal Tourette's of shivers
The overnight toe stalagmites
The nasal passageway rivers
The eyes cut blind by the white
The lips of spittle-ice slivers
Suggest it's an unequal fight

A soggy you comes to my door
A nose inside seven coats
We hug as you drip on the floor
Your boots developing moats
First kiss, through layers, a chore
Romance can be tough when you're soaked

I conjure up tea and we rest
By the heater's inadequate whirr
You whine about work you detest
Then refer to your boss with a slur
I listen while doing my best
To be your therm donor preferred

Microwave something for food
Telly for passing the time
Outside the snow is renewed
As inside so ditto the wine
You suggest activities lewd
Just for the heat they provide

After our strenuous plays
As spent as an arsonist's match
We lie in a blanketed haze
All cares now given dispatch
Drifting off in a daze
Where visions of summer may hatch

What is hell? That's easy to say
Hell is cold, it's white, and outside
What is heaven? No need to pray
It's having you here by my side
Winter just one of the ways
I'm reminded of my paradise

Jilted

Though all the hours we've shared have been divine
Now must I say farewell, and take my leave
I thought we'd be together for all time
But now I know this was not meant to be

A man must make his choice, which can be hard
Since love's a game of rules not always fair
I know you have been good, done me no harm
But now another's heart has won my care

Yes, we were good together, and my arms
Did often hold you in protective style
I've no complaints, you still have all your charms
Nor have you strayed, betrayed or practised guile

You've always been there for me, day and night
As faithful as the line is to the rule
Yet now my love's aligned to different sights
I trust, in time, you will not think me cruel

For all I loved to hold you, stroke, caress
Your gentle curves, and have you sing for me
Now there's another whom I must confess
I do prefer, I state it honestly

With us, love's melody just seemed to flow
Alas, it seems we've reached the final bar
Yet she is now my choice, to her I go
So then farewell, my true, much-loved guitar

Kiss Met

It was the kiss that crystallised
All knowing of the need inside
Distilled the dreams 'til then denied
Of love's reality defined

It was the kiss that lit the fire
Of two lifetimes' long-sought desire
Commanded two heartbeats conspire
In search of all romance admires

It was the kiss that gave us flight
Into the fast release of night
One secret touch, one shared respite
That has become one world of light

Sausalito

In the morning in Sausalito
The light was soft, lazy gold
We parked by the bay and we wandered
Through streets that never get old

You pointed to places you knew
From stories you lived long ago
Told me of little girl secrets and dreams
You chose to never let go

On Bonita we stopped by a gallery
You found a painting you liked
Then posed like the girl in the picture, and laughed
Such a beautiful sight

At mid-day in Sausalito
With iced tea, watching the birds
We twisted ourselves into knots for a while
Kissing our thoughts into words

We mixed our brilliant decision
From a palette of safe and insane
Our fingers entwined in a lattice of faith
Barely noticed the rain

In the evening in Sausalito
The light fell quickly away
We sheltered down by the bridge for a while
Said all the good things to say

We named stars for one another
Gifted our love to their light
Then you gave yourself to the shadows
We promised we never would write

The ruin of love can be done
In ten scratched years or a day
But the picture that never gets painted
Is the picture that nothing can fade

Sanctuary

My worst and my best
My whole and my part
My know and my guess
My completion, my start
My more and my less
My science, my art
All these, the possess
Of your sanctuary heart

Cut To The Chase

A's for Admire
As I surely do
B is for Beautiful
That's surely you

C we'll miss out
D is for Dance
S is for Sex...
                    ...any chance?

Insight

Seductive lines such as the poet may write
Hold him to ransom by their crafted rhyme
As map to land, they offer clear insight
Knowledge that, applied, saves faith and time

Each writer by his trade is rendered true
Sins, flaws and all show up in words expressed
Pray then how should he start liaisons new
Except if he by sweet perfection's blessed?

All love prefers a flawless path to 'Yes'
Rejecting suitors if perceived as marred
Enamoured hearts, in truth, do first assess
Sincerity of virtue and regard

Since this be so, romantic verses laid
Oft when they would impress, merely offend
Unless, that is, love's truth instead be weighed
Less by the writer's arts than by his ends

Unfinished

In fires that teach the heart its fear
Too scared to bring each other near
No matter how we dry the tears
I swear this love does not end here

In silence where the doubts can play
With all the words two souls can say
No matter what it takes to stay
I swear we will not end this way

In shadows where the rage can bite
As anger rips the fading light
No matter how we make it right
I swear we will not end this night

In echoes of scorched trust review
From rights and wrongs of shattered truth
No matter what we have to do
I swear I shall keep loving you

Trick Of Love

This is the trick of love
Sense-whip and quick of love
Sly little slick subtle skin-nicking prick above
Reason and treason, time or design
That steals away hearts; the sign of the crime
Being flowers and verses, passions and curses
Hours sublime of the best and the worst
That we know how to be, ever will see
Of the her and the he
Spent lovers covered in passion's debris

Naked as new but aged with the truth
Cut with the lessons of revel and rue
Thousands of yesterdays lost in the head
Crossed in the said and the spoken and thought
The should and the couldn't and didn't and ought
Wrongs upon rights, days upon mights
Will she and won't he and doesn't time fly
Each kiss a bit nearer to death than the last
Yet seems to renew, seems to include
Fresh living, fresh blood, fresh chances to play
At what would life be, if life were okay
If all of the thorns just melted away
So we were just sunlight and chocolate and lay
In heaven, that is, in each other's arms
Suffused with the charms and the calm of it all
Smiling, touching, heeding the call
Of the happiest possible fall

Lost in a paradise fable for two
Maison me and you
An adequate crew
For adventures incautious, salacious and wild
As tame as tarantulas, rapacious and child-
-like in our search, in each other's eyes
For that silence, most prized
When we know that we count, we matter, we're real
That someone, somewhere can actually feel
If we're there or not, and knows how to make
The tea just right, and is willing to take
Whatever love brings
The be and the stings

Someone to share life's gems and jewels
The important things, the karma fuel
Like photographs taken ages ago
Far too embarrassing ever to show
Songs that we sing though we don't know the words
Pillow talk plans uniquely absurd
The secret of making really good haupia
DIY triumphs that lead to a loud cheer
Treasure and secrets (some of them crude)
Taxis and tandems, unreasonable moods
Our paradise bed, or new kitchen table
That turns out to be not quite as stable
As first we assumed, not quite the robust
Support we sought for our intrepid lust
But at least as we end up sprawled on the floor
Killing ourselves with giggles galore
Studying bruises not there before
It's with someone we like and life isn't a bore

(continued >)

This is the trick of love, the loving of tricks
We play on ourselves, we use it to fix
The problems, the worries, the bruising and rips
Trips, stumbles, stones and sticks
That ruin the people we're trying to be
Those perfect visions of you and of me

So here is my hand, which you don't have to take
But you might, and you'll find this me isn't fake
That I promise I'm real, can't promise more
I really don't care how loudly you snore
(Not yet, anyway), because your best trick
That you do very well — red-finger-nailed click! —
Is happening to be, just as you are
The brightest star
That I could love, and if that's good enough
Let's do a bit more of this 'fall in love' stuff

Nobody

Lamplight ellipses
On dusk renewed snow
You walk to the heartbeat
Of silence you know
A child to the world
In a desert of rain
A searcher for peace
In Circus Insane

Chilled city pavements
Your carpets of ice
You cling to the memories
Of plans for this life
None knowing better
The kick or the kiss
Myths that we trust
Or chances we miss

Crystals refracted
By bright neon lies
You breathe like a ghost
Eyelashes trimmed white
Lost to the scars
Of your beauty's despair
Snowflakes for a shroud
And always… nobody there

Circle of Strife

Listen dear, about last night
I was wrong, and you were right
All those stupid things I said
Were wrong, unfair, I lost my head
I didn't want an argument
That truly wasn't my intent
I offer my apology
It is sincere, I hope you'll be
Forgiving of my dumb mistakes
What's more no matter what it takes
I'll make it up to you, my love
I can't apologise enough

I'm sorry that I raised my voice
I should have made a different choice
There probably was a better way
To point out how you ruined the day
More tact was needed, I can see
A little more diplomacy… what?

Look, when I say "ruined the day"
It's not meant in a nasty way
But, you know, let's not deny
You really messed it up big-time
The facts, my dear, are plain to see
What do you mean, "Don't 'my dear' me"?
Look, all I'm saying... don't be like that
Can't we have a peaceful chat?

Yes, I did apologise
But don't imagine that implies
I take the blame for your mistakes
Because I don't, for goodness sake
I'm really not attacking you
I'm merely pointing out the truth
I don't think it should be a crime
To point out that from time to time
You get things wrong, it's just a fact
You mess up this or mess up that
Look, really there's no need for this
Let's make up with a hug and kiss...
What? Why the sudden "Go to hell?"
I know I get things wrong as well

Okay, well look, I really tried
I said I'm sorry, apologised
I really can't do any more
Where are you going? Why slam the door?

(continued >)

That's typical of you, that is!
I try and be nice, all hug and kiss
But no, you'd rather have a row
Like some hysterical whiny cow
It's strange because in the books I read
They seemed to think Hitler was dead
What's more…

Oh, you're back
No, I didn't call you a name
I said "like", which isn't quite the same
The Hitler thing was just a joke
I'm sorry, I felt a bit provoked

Yes, it makes sense to assume
I wouldn't want to share a room
With a cow, so of course, instead
I'll just make up the sofa bed
You've brought a blanket, very kind
You didn't have to throw it, mind
At least a goodnight kiss to show…
Slam! I'll take that as a no
So, that's it then, I'll sleep down here
Very well, goodnight my dear

- - -

Listen dear, about last night…

Yours

You breathe and I see
You talk and I track
All that I ever wanted and lacked
Made real, brought back and
Flown to my eyes, shown to my heart
Like every prize I chased from the start

It's a glory attack, romantical flak
Clipping my wings, the bullets they sing
As they singe, bring me down
Mind spinning around
You capture me, rapture me
Watch as I stall, so helplessly fall
In the sea of your curious smile, without trial
Caught and detained
Full rank and name
Possibly framed (but it's all in the game)
So I'm locked by the chains
Of your fizzical brain
Your lips, hot kisses, calculus fine
Your sines so divine
The happiest captive of all
Slowest to call for the keys of release
That I hope I never shall reach

What you create
What you give shape to
Fashion and form that I must relate to
Is a magical madrigal
Maze of crazes
Madnesses lyrical
Mostly romantical
Wrapped in a dawn erasing all cynical
Trace, your skin a raw heat
That melts all of me, slowly defeats
All thoughts, all time, all denial, all past
Distresses and guesses that now I confess
Were never the love that I need

By your passion, your pride in motions seductive
You trap my devotions with kisses instructive
Of love gratified
Heaven derived
Yours, alone yours
For a million tides

Questions Of The Day

Has a cheese ever mastered the cello
Do astronauts wear knitted suits?
Was Heidi a big bearded fellow
Do whales survive chiefly on fruit?

Are bridges elastic and treacle
Do chemists wear nitrogen socks?
Are inches and tons about equal
Was Picasso the true King of Rock?

Is physics for things that are fizzy
With unclear physics for fuzzy?
Are dissidents usually dizzy
Do I always find a great rhyme?

Could a daffodil one day be President
Do foxes make boxes from bricks?
Is Gandhi an icon of decadence
Did I forget to put 'socks' in line six?

The answer for all is most surely the same
As for my two questions the last
Did I not need my fun-loving lover today
And as lovers, are we poorly cast?

Health

Though outwardly it seems I've health enough
Not so, for this my heart like all alive
Must fade if sun and water long denied
Yet knows no source of either but your love
Thus takes my heart its toll each dawn and dusk
Which serve but to extend its wearied blight
Make all the world one desert, ever night
With no reprieve save's granted by your touch
Yet have I equal cause to curse and bless
This passion's flay of twin-locked pain and grace
Since I'd not miss of which I'd had no taste
Would feel a lesser pain, if had felt less
True love invokes its own reversed guise
For parting's no distress if together is no prize

Renewal

Now words are found not worth the breath to say
All speech is useless to this place, this hour
For all's complete, this love's long-wintered wait
Has thawed and so set free love's finest flower
Some forty days and nights, each coldly dressed
Has droned this rank embraceless term its course
Of trapped affection, skin left uncaressed
With love denied its flow from mirrored source
Yet burned love's fragile flame this long chill through
Sustained by knowledge of this hour's birth
Which now, at touch, will kindle love's renew
Such that we lose all time and reign this Earth
So make all poets fools, my Love, all words at once dismiss
Say all that's worth to say of love with single, silent kiss

Forever

The sickly sun leaves the faint rags of its pride
In a farewell of crimson on faltering gold
Restless, the river's shared whispers confide
Their cascading echoes of stories untold

Tower Bridge offers a sentinel stance
On Potters Fields park and battleship chained
Lovers and workers drift into the trance
Of their ritual dances and freedoms regained

She follows the early spring easterly breeze
To the bench that provides a view of the Tower
"Well, I'm here", she says, to herself and the trees
Once again murmurs the place and the hour

She clutches the note that caused all the tears
Two scribbled lines with her name at the end
Scans every footstep and face that comes near
Delusion and shadows play pricks of pretend

Each false-alarm figure's a cruel passing jest
On her heart that's afire with wishes and prayer
She waits, the one thing she has always done best
For the one who must hear what she has to share

She straightens her collar, then tugs at her cuff
Each minute that passes a windowless cell
Trapped in the maze of how long is enough
To wait for the answers she promised to tell

Around her, anonymous faces pass by
Fleeting, translucent, she watches the flow
Invisible to them, she nonetheless tries
To warn of the cold and the deep undertow

The evening grows into a chorus of clues
He's not going to show for this fix of romance
So hard to accept, such love to refuse
Who could deny this ghost of a chance?

She turns to the make-believe face that she sees
Alongside on the bench, and whispers her words
"I will love you forever, please try to believe
All that I asked was a chance to be heard"

Silence surrounds her in fast-fading light
As the air lends a chill to the close of the day
"If you'd been here I could have made everything right
Then I wouldn't have wanted to go far away"

She stands up and strolls to the riverside wall
Looks over the note, rips once, rips twice
Scatters the pieces, they drift and they fall
To the waters below in ordained sacrifice

She heads for the bridge, resolved, unafraid
The city starts settling down for the night
Lovers and workers drift into the shade
Trains become busy and stars become bright

None notice or hear her, none see her face
All pass through the sadness she cannot betray
Tomorrow, the same, every step she'll retrace
As she's done every night since passing away

Dark Eyes

She can walk upon water with tricks of belief
Caress of an angel, the hand of a thief
She can fracture a sadness on the rock of her heart
Then waltz around madness
With steps she has known from the start

She can vanquish the silence of indifferent minds
With the kiss of contrivances always denied
She never needs threats but she carries the shields
Of secret regrets
On the face her reflection conceals

A soul mate to strangers and mystery to friends
A book without pages, whirl without end
Through destiny's chains she can slip like the mist
Untouched by the rains
That lesser hearts always resist

The charm of all seasons in flames around ice
Dark Eyes gives only the worst of advice
The best of all glories in plastic on gold
Dark Eyes has the stories
I waited so long to be told

Saying love is the signal to go on her way
She left me the memories I try not to play
Dark Eyes in her treason neglected to say
How gods love or reason
Could somehow persuade her to stay

Kinder Blade

This is the safer prison cell
This is the kinder blade
To keep my distance, never tell
What love I had to trade

This is the wound more quickly healed
The scar that sooner fades
To see that sunlight smile and steal
One glance, then walk away

It's not for fear — I'd face the pain
I don't find that so hard
We all survive, all play the game
Re-mix and match the cards

I just don't want to weld the link
Between that searing flame
And you, and all the love I think
To wrap around your name

Though sad, pathetic, it may seem
To not pursue the find
To have the sweet ten-second dream
Then leave it all behind

Yet I will own the peaceful prize
I need, more than they see
To never know the endless night
You take your love from me

Seasons

Come Spring, then will you walk with me?
As frost's clear casket's cracked
By sun's slant-razored dawning
On life anew untrapped

Come Summer, will you walk with me?
While hue's unstemmed cascade
Casts light new-gashed, fresh-scented
Through playful, long-lived days

Come Fall, then will you walk with me?
As mist, thick-tendrilled, breathes
Some stealth-unfurled translucent veils
To catch hushed fallen leaves

Come Winter, will you walk with me?
All's silhouette-craft strokes,
Slow-sealed in crystalled cadence
As silent flake, on silent flake, soft falls the new-wept snow

Good friend, then will you walk with me
As we find paths enough
To make our kiss of trust endure
Through all seasons of love?

Dawning

This dawn brings only darkness more
This fire no warmth provides
No sound can salve the silence charred
That chains the loss inside

One fragile wish, to count, to care
All cinders now, all dust
Settled, undisturbed, new coat
For this defeated trust

An angry dullness cracks the air
At comprehension's wake
A time to view the guts, hook-ripped
From faith and other fakes

Then falls the foolish lash of whys
The rancid swill of hows
Descent, descent all fathomless
Through traps of bracken vows

What power you had to sinter joy
From my defeated days
To smile and love and kiss-transmute
Dark ice to Eden's haze

Rain Listening

Night's fallen on a world grown far too vast
For souls unmatched
Touched only by the distances
That separate themselves and whispered words
From voices missed

Rain's falling on a world grown far too cold
For souls dismayed
Cocooned in night's black oxygen
Through which they stare to fathom purpose
For their still unprized affection

I feel their questions
I feel the stifled scream
Of their unsparing aspiration
Detecting in the rain
The soft unfading echoes of their whys

Then terrorised, within
The sweet pacific chalice of your love
Your awkward dream-slack arm across my chest
I take uncounted hours
To look at you
To gently kiss your hair, and practise my
Rain listening

Girl Of Two Worlds

I travelled by wish and by moonlight
To the girl of two worlds, who wept
Trapped by a goblin of night
In a chamber where fear never slept

She cried, "I am lost and resigned
For the goblin will not set me free
Unless all the answers I find
To the riddles he's set before me"

To the girl of two worlds, I did say
That magic was love with a twist
I would free her, and love her always
Each tear replaced with a kiss

She looked with hope in her heart
"How I wish you could make it so
But the goblin says I can't depart
Unless by the dawn I can show…"

A world that spins along the ground
A stream that flows remaining still
A bell that chimes without a sound
A seed that grows above the hills

A hawk that climbs but once a year
A rose that's made of fire and metal
A golden ring of luck and cheer
A game that's played upon a petal

A bee that stings catching the dew
A web that's spun by cherry trees
A bird that calls singing no tune
A dog that runs from sky to seas
Rains that fall so all is truth

I said, "You shall have your desire"
Then summoned the goblin appear
Who mocked us, and cackled with fire
"No mortal shall ever leave here!"

But I stared at the goblin's green eyes
Declaring, "This day she goes free!
Your spells I do scorn and despise
She will leave this chamber with me!"

Said the grimacing goblin, "Not so!
The spell and the contract prevail
To be free, these things you must show
Before this enchantment can fail"

"Very well", I replied, and incanted
A weaving of magical signs
Then a flash of magic enchanted
Revealed the relaying of lines:

A world that spins

Along the ground: a stream that flows
Remaining still: a bell that chimes
Without a sound: a seed that grows
Above the hills: a hawk that climbs

But once a year: a rose that's made
Of fire and metal: a golden ring
Of luck and cheer: a game that's played
Upon a petal: a bee that stings

Catching the dew: a web that's spun
By cherry trees: a bird that calls
Singing no tune: a dog that runs
From sky to seas: rains that fall

So all is truth

(continued >)

With a terrible scream and a roar
With a thunderous shaking of sound
The goblin sank into the floor
Dissolving right into the ground

Then his chamber of gobliny horridness
Was gone in a flash of green smoke
So the spell of lonely unhappiness
For once and forever, I broke

The girl of two worlds and I flew
To a garden of magic and jade
Where we made for ourselves a life new
With tea and white chocolatey cakes

To the girl of two worlds, I did say
That magic was love with a twist
I freed her, to love her always
Now every day she is kissed

Puzzle Poems Section

A dozen examples of what happens when romantic poetry collides with the curious and contrived concoction of content craftily concealed.

The next twelve poems are all puzzle poems. Each of them contains a concealed phrase or message. As you can see, the first of these puzzle poems is called 'Mirage'. At first glance, it may appear to be just a normal poem. Before you read any further, can you find the hidden message it contains?

- - -

Here's the answer to the 'Mirage' poem. If you look at just the *first* letter of each line you will see that they spell out a message: 'Make Love With Me'. This is called an acrostic and it is the simplest type of puzzle poem in this section.

The concealed messages always conform to a fixed rule or pattern (e.g. 'take the last letter of every second word') but they become progressively more difficult to find. Some of the puzzle poems contain small clues about how to find the hidden message or messages. However, most of the clues are rather weak and some are simply misleading.

There are twelve puzzle poems in all. The last one, called 'Infatuation', is the most fiendishly difficult one and took a *very* long time to construct. The solutions are provided in the next section of the book.

Mirage

Mysterious paths are lain for lover's thoughts
All strewn with sly enigmas, subtle traps
Kissed hearts do fight bewilderment's onslaught
Erased of reason, knowledge, rule or facts
Let this be so, for though this mirrored hall
Of mind mirage may sweetly tantalise
Value it less we would if love were all
Encompassed in what's swiftly analysed
Walk with me, then, into conundrum's lair
Intake of intuition's true perplex
Track these words, and trust to what we'll share
Here asked of you, if you would but suspect
Make of these lines your study and your play
Escape their lie to see the lying craved

On Offer

Good truth alone may chart where hearts align
No map being fit to answer love's location
In that affection's force does not opine
To deem one single place its full vocation

Such is romance it never can espouse
An hour or date as sum of its excess
Love shapes itself in time-transcendent vows
Respecting of no calendar's express

Elusive love no words fairly reflect
Verse being but paper jail to passion's light
Each heart sustains its eloquent aspect
Even when speech succumbs to silent sighs

View well such traits of love as here are taught
Observe from first to last and twice impressed
Lest all I strive to give should come to naught
And slip your grasp, for want of being guessed

Intent

No dark seductive secrets I maintain
In being overt I state clearest intent
These words I therefore lay before you plain
In that I would thereby win your consent

I ask one thing, one gift alone of you
Long sought since first I gazed into your eyes
Wish for it less I would if less I knew
That it would be a taste of paradise

Short is this life such that virtue dictates
To win what bliss we may, not to prevent
Wrong choices lead nowhere but lonely state
Therefore I do suggest you should assent

It is a waste to block this honest thirst
Both wit and passion plead do not deny
The ends so clearly stated from the first
Fear not desire's truth, but grant this lie

Desires

There is no need to waste each other's time
For it's as clear as ever it could be
Unless you see some paths to which I'm blind
I can't predict romance for you and me

Harsh though it sounds, I mean no disrespect
This truth is what it is, no blame attached
One loves or one loves not, we can't expect
Close ties where hearts are not so closely matched

Desire is strange, not bound by law or sense
Skilled though we both may be in loving arts
I cannot see the point of sad pretence
As honest words best serve the loving heart

Stoop not to think my nature's not to care
I should protest this lie and so would you
Let's not resort to slander, so unfair
We both are good, just not of loving hue

Extract from this, my dear, my strong desires
I place them, five in all, in open view
Locked in true lines that may alternate lie
I own they are what I'd most do with you

Very soon these acts I trust we'll share
Receive my gifts, all five, of deepest care

One Act

The heart implies its needs in sundry ways
Kind words and gentle touch to name but two
Such that desire may amply be conveyed
Yet still permit discretion's gentler view

Unsubtle declarations lack finesse
Nuance makes finer paths for lovers' play
Yet do not think me coy, for I express
Exactly what I want, and need, and pray

Doubt not the clarity of my intention
But 'clear' and 'pure' are not to be confused
My wish is plain, no need of circumvention
It would be such a shame if you refused

Open your heart, my love, to this request
See how I simply state this passion's fire
In letters neat, from ends to centre set
One act, one place, being all that I desire

Eye To Eye

Eye to eye, and face to face, let truth be plainly said
We'll waste no time or spirit on a bed of broken hearts
All will lose when losers all give start to what they dread
Ways are always found to shed the blood when love departs

Slow to love I surely am if you're the choice in view
Few reasons for the tango two arise where you're concerned
With kindness let this choice be spurned there'll be no me and you
Keys and locks are best refused when trust is not returned

Says this lover to the would-be-loved not so this time
And hold it not so much a crime as mercy given rein
Affect no sad complexion, neither strain a tear sublime
Shun love not of condition prime these lines soundly explain

Fulfilment

This is no time for words of grand oration
Let's banish eloquence, I am inclined
Exactly to declare by this notation
A single wish you'll grant, if you'll be kind

Express agreement and I'll demonstrate
By word and deed for months or even years
Your choice is right, and we shall orchestrate
Unrivalled love, as all that's right reveres

Stay your objections, please, they'll not impress
Dull, dreary fables fail love's true extent
Be braver, wiser, find your path to 'yes'
Beware those chaste, whom being not chased, repent

Enter, I plead, this pact of good advice
Know that you may select in– or outdoors
For, as my first and last do here devise
All that I seek's fulfilment — mine and yours

Patient Friend

Cafés and lunches around the West End
Nice chats about funny internet trends
Pleasant strolls out by the Serpentine lake
Each of these pleasures I gladly will take

Seashores and guided tours down into caves
Mad nights of dancing at out of town raves
Keep fit aerobics and workouts on bikes
Lots of these things that we share, I like

Very late parties with far too much booze
Wine tasting sessions and shopping for shoes
Theatres, galleries full of art treasures
You share with me so many aspects of leisure

Topical lectures and pottery classes
Niche-appeal fiction and Glastonbury passes
Ghost walks, casinos and 'Open Mic' nights
These are all pastimes that bring me delight

Cake stalls in Camden, Tai-Chi for beginners
Night-time safaris, Chef's Table dinners
Plays by political refugee groups
Easter egg hunts, there's so much to do!

Seeing how slowly TV shows are taped
Making fresh pasta in interesting shapes
Kew Gardens visits, Brown's afternoon tea
Looking at star maps, there's plenty to see

Vestibule painting (magnolia and plum)
Wimbledon tickets, a first bungee jump
These brilliant activities fill every day
You brighten my life, except in one way

To be honest, my friend, not that I'd be crude
Night times, I feel, could perhaps be improved
Ghastly idea, you may say, nonetheless
These lines, politely, twice state my request

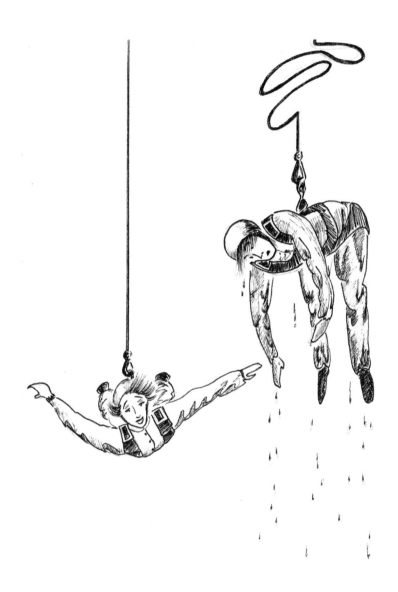

No Hidden Message

To hide within some verse a secret phrase
Entails repeated mangling of sense
Each instance of a line contrived or crazed
Signals nifty word-twisting intense

One happy minute noting choice absurd
In details such as odd vocab or rhyme
Duly extricates all hidden words
No master sleuthing needed for this crime

Each solver knows to search for choices strained
So all my deft concealment's bound to fail
Great effort though I make, the fact remains
I'll never win, like zebras fighting whales

This hopeless trade I'll therefore leave behind
I shall conceal no message in this verse
Plain ordinary lines, I think you'll find
Each made to be a secret hunter's curse

Love's Deceit

Expect no care from me, for I remain
Averse to your supposed charm so sweet
The truth is I prefer my single ways
To problematic ties (such as you'd be)

Fair Lady trust I have no thoughts for you
Too frail you are in heart, in looks, in mind
Please seek romance elsewhere, I bid you to
The less to waste your hours, or squander mine

Part will I now, for I've no cause to stay
Yet there's no art to find a parting word
All's said in 'goodbye' that requires the say
While 'farewell' is all now that needs be heard

Please not to doubt these words so plainly scored
Contain fair invocation of the truth
Each line a greater than the one before
In conveying clearly how I look on you

Integrity

Trust reflects an image twice on rested lovers' play
Reciprocating all the while, faith being the faithful way
Exalted love, our virtue's end, recycles its own clay

All love inspires alliance rich, our bond a wealth we've earned
Close hearts enjoy a trust well-taught and — in each kiss — re-learned
Honour and romance proclaim your love being mine returned

Each view I love is but of you, and how you lie with me
Reach out to this eternal need for love's integrity
You offer understanding's peace, which now, at last, I see

Infatuation

The summer sun we spent as lovers do
Wrapped in the shaded leisure of our care
But now these days of idle dreams are through
As cooler rays draw forth a calmer view
And gloomy clouds eclipse our sweet affair

Mourn as we may, no truth could be more clear
What we have had is now a fading light
For all that we may share a fallen tear
To think upon each twilight kiss held dear
Time has run out on this impassioned flight

You told me faithful love should never end
But I know love is just one season's play
The arts of love we've shared do not depend
On arid visions such as fools defend
Of one infatuation for all days

Thus now we part, let's not play or pretend
The good love goes, the tough love takes its place
To you I say farewell my lover friend
I offer just one hope that I intend:
Use fewer letters and my wish you'll trace

This is the last of the twelve puzzle poems. Of course, there is the distinct possibility that some of the other poems in this book also contain hidden messages of one kind or another. Just because something isn't labelled as a puzzle doesn't mean it isn't one. Who can say for sure?

Puzzle Poems Solutions

The next few pages contain the solutions to
the twelve puzzle poems. Do not proceed any
further unless you want to see the answers!

Mirage - Solution

Mysterious paths are lain for lover's thoughts
All strewn with sly enigmas, subtle traps
Kissed hearts do fight bewilderment's onslaught
Erased of reason, knowledge, rule or facts
Let this be so, for though this mirrored hall
Of mind mirage may sweetly tantalise
Value it less we would if love were all
Encompassed in what's swiftly analysed
Walk with me, then, into conundrum's lair
Intake of intuition's true perplex
Track these words, and trust to what we'll share
Here asked of you, if but you would suspect
Make of these lines your study and your play
Escape their lie to see the lying craved

- - -

Key: Take the first letter of each line. These letters spell:

MAKE LOVE WITH ME

The small clue is the phrase 'Escape their lie'. How do words normally lie on a page? Horizontally. To 'escape their lie' suggests trying a different direction, i.e. vertically.

On Offer - Solution

Good truth alone may chart where hearts **A**lign
No map being fit to answer love's **L**ocation
In that affection's force does not **O**pine
To deem one single place its full **V**ocation

Such is romance it never can **E**spouse
An hour or date as sum of its **E**xcess
Love shapes itself in time-transcendent **V**ows
Respecting of no calendar's **E**xpress

Elusive love no words fairly **R**eflect
Verse being but paper jail to passion's **L**ight
Each heart sustains its eloquent **A**spect
Even though speech succumb to silent **S**ighs

View well such traits of love as here are **T**aught
Observe from first to last and twice **I**mpressed
Lest all I strive to give should come to **N**aught
And slip your grasp, for want of being **G**uessed

- - -

Key: Take the first letter of the first word in each line. These letters spell:

A LOVE EVERLASTING

However, the letters are in reverse order, so they need to be read from the last line to the first line.

Then, take the first letter of the *last* word in each line. These spell the same message.

Hence the same message is concealed twice within the same lines. The small clue is that the message is 'twice impressed' within the lines but can only be seen if the reader observes 'from first to last'.

Intent - Solution

NO dark seductive secrets I maintain
SiN makes a richer brew by clear intent
ThesE words I therefore lay before you plain
IN that I would thereby win your consent

I ask one thing, one gift alone of you
LonG sought since first I gazed into your eyes
WisH for it less I would if less I knew
ThaT it would be a taste of paradise

ShorT is this life such that virtue dictates
TO win what bliss we may, not to prevent
WronG choices lead nowhere but lonely state
ThereforE I do suggest you should assent

IT is a waste to block this honest thirst
BotH wit and passion plead do not deny
ThE ends so clearly stated from the first
FeaR not desire's truth, but grant this lie

- - -

Key: Take the *last* letter of the *first* word in each line. These letters spell:

ONE NIGHT TOGETHER

The only vague clue provided is the line 'The *ends* [the last letters] so clearly stated *from the first* [from the first words]'.

Desires - Solution

There is no need to waste each other's time
FOr it's as clear as ever it could be
Unless you see some paths to which I'm blind
I Can't predict romance for you and me

Harsh though it sounds, I mean no disrespect
THis truth is what it is, no blame attached
One loves or one loves not, we can't expect
CLose ties where hearts are not so closely matched

Desire is strange, not bound by law or sense
SKilled though we both may be in loving arts
I cannot see the point of sad pretence
AS honest words best serve the loving heart

Stoop not to think my nature's not to care
I Should protest this lie and so would you
Let's not resort to slander, so unfair
WE both are good, just not of loving hue

Extract from this, my dear, my strong desires
I Place them, five in all, in open view
Locked in true lines that may alternate lie
I Own they are what I'd most do with you

Very soon these acts I trust we'll share
REceive my gifts, all five, of deepest care

- - -

Key: Extract the first letter of every odd line and the second letter of every even line. These letters spell:

TOUCH HOLD KISS SLEEP LOVE

These are the five acts referred to. The only vague clue provided is the line 'Locked in true lines that may alternate lie'.

One Act - Solution

The heart implies its needs in sundry ways
Kind words and gentle touch to name but two
Such that desire may amply be conveyed
Yet still permit discretion's gentler view

Unsubtle declarations lack finesse
Nuance makes finer paths for lovers' play
Yet do not think me coy, for I express
Exactly what I want, and need, and pray

Doubt not the clarity of my intention
But 'clear' and 'pure' are not to be confused
My wish is plain, no need of circumvention
It would be such a shame if you refused

Open your heart, my love, to this request
See how I simply state this passion's fire
In letters neat, from ends to centre set
One act, one place, being all that I desire

- - -

Key: Take the first letters of each line. These letters spell:

TKSY UNYE DBMI OSIO

These letters have to be read in a specific sequence, like this:
First line, last line
Second line, second from last line
Third line, third from last line
Fourth line, fourth from last line ...and so on.

When read in this way, they spell:

TO KISS YOU IN MY BED

The only vague clue provided is the phrase 'from ends to centre set'.

Eye To Eye – Solution

Eye to eye, and face to face, let truth be plainly said
We'll waste no time or spirit on a bed of broken hearts
All is lost when losers all give start to what they dread
Ways are always found to shed the blood when love departs
Slow to love I surely am if you're the choice in view
Few reasons for the tango two arise where you're concerned
With kindness let this choice be spurned there'll be no me and you
Keys and locks are best refused when trust is not returned
Says this lover to the would be loved not so this time
And hold it not so much a crime as mercy given rein
Affect no sad complexion, neither strain a tear sublime
Shun love not of condition prime these lines soundly explain

- - -

Key: Take the first word of each line:

Eye we'll all ways slow few with keys says and affect shun

These words can be pronounced in such a way that they are close to:

I WILL ALWAYS LOVE YOU WITH KISSES AND AFFECTION

The only slight clue is the reference to "*soundly* explain".

Only the first words in each line matter with regard to the secret message. All the other words are irrelevant. However, I tried to make this look like a real poem with a few elements that jarred or seemed unusual, as if *they* were the awkward compromises that indicate concealment of some kind. I also hoped the reference to 'prime' would encourage some solvers to think in terms of prime numbers.

Fulfilment - Solution

This is no time for words of grand **O**ration
Let's banish eloquence, I am **I**nclined
Exactly to declare by this **N**otation
A single wish you'll grant, if you'll be **K**ind

Express agreement and I'll **D**emonstrate
By word and deed for months or even **Y**ears
Your choice is right, and we shall **O**rchestrate
Unrivalled love, as all that's right **R**everes

Stay your objections, please, they'll not **I**mpress
Dull, dreary fables fail love's true **E**xtent
Be braver, wiser, find your path to '**Y**es'
Beware those chaste, whom being not chased, **R**epent

Enter, I plead, this pact of good **A**dvice
Know that you may select in- or **O**utdoors
For, as my first and last do here **D**evise
All that I seek's fulfilment — mine and **Y**ours

- - -

Key: Take the initial letters of the first and last words of each line.
These letters spell:

TO LIE NAKED BY YOUR SIDE BY BREAK OF DAY

The clue is the phrase 'For as my first and last do here devise'.

Patient Friend – Solution

CAfés and lunches around the West End
NIce chats about funny internet trends
PLeasant strolls out by the Serpentine lake
EAch of these pleasures I gladly will take

SEashores and guided tours down into caves
MAd nights and dancing at out of town raves
KEep fit aerobics and workouts on bikes
LOts of these things that we share, I like

VEry late parties with far too much booze
WIne tasting sessions and shopping for shoes
THeatres, galleries full of art treasures
YOU share with me so many aspects of leisure

TOpical lectures and pottery classes
Niche-appeal fiction and Glastonbury passes
GHost walks, casinos and 'Open Mic' nights
These are all pastimes that bring me delight

CAke stalls in Camden, Tai-Chi for beginners
NIght-time safaris, Chef's Table dinners
PLays by political refugee groups
EAster egg hunts, there's so much to do!

SEeing the way that TV shows are taped
MAking fresh pasta in interesting shapes
KEw Gardens visits, Brown's afternoon tea
LOoking at star maps, there's plenty to see

VEstibule painting (magnolia and plum)
WImbledon tickets, a first bungee jump
THese brilliant activities fill every day
YOU brighten my life, except in *one* way

TO be honest, my friend, not that I'd be crude
Night times, I feel, could perhaps be improved
GHastly idea, you may say, nonetheless
These lines, politely, twice state my request

(*continued >*)

(Solution for 'Patient Friend' continued)

Key: Take the first *two* letters from each line. There are two exceptions. The first *three* letters are required from lines 12 and 24 (to make the word 'you') and only *one* letter is required from lines 16 and 32 (to provide a single letter 't' in either case). These letters spell the same phrase twice:

CAN I PLEASE MAKE LOVE WITH YOU TONIGHT

Why does the pattern get interrupted with 'you' in this way? Because otherwise I would have to find two different words starting with 'Ut....' and I'm not sure there are any apart from 'utter'. I would also have to find words beginning with 'ht', which don't exist.

I tried concealing many other words and phrases but it's difficult to find a phrase of suitable length that can be split into two-letter pairs, each of which can serve as the start of a line of verse.

No Hidden Message - Solution

To Hide within some verse a secret phrase
Entails Repeated mangling of sense
Each Instance of a line contrived or crazed
Signals Nifty word-twisting intense

One Happy minute noting choice absurd
In Details such as odd vocab or rhyme
Duly Extricates all hidden words
No Master sleuthing needed for this crime

Each Solver knows to search for choices strained
So All my deft concealment's bound to fail
Great Effort though I make, the fact remains
I'll Never win, like zebras fighting whales

This Hopeless trade I'll therefore leave behind
I Shall conceal no message in this verse
Plain Ordinary lines, I think you'll find
Each Made to be a secret hunter's curse

- - -

Key: Take the first letter from the first and second words in each line. These letters spell:

THERE IS NO HIDDEN MESSAGE IN THIS POEM

It is curiously satisfying to construct a poem in which the hidden message denies its own existence.

Love's Deceit - Solution

Expect no care from me, for I remain
AVerse to your supposed charm so sweet
ThE truth is I prefer my single ways
To pRoblematic ties (such as you'd be)

Fair Lady trust I have no thoughts for you
Too frAil you are in heart, in looks, in mind
Please Seek romance elsewhere, I bid you to
The less To waste your hours, or squander mine

Part will I now, for I've no cause to stay
Yet there's No art to find a parting word
All's said in 'goodbye' that requires the say
While 'farewell' is all that now needs be heard

Please not to dOubt these words so plainly scored
Contain fair inVocation of the truth
Each line a greatEr than the one before
In conveying cleaRly how I look on you

- - -

Key: Take the 1st letter of line 1; the 2nd letter of line 2; the 3rd letter of line 3… and so on. These letters spell:

EVERLASTING LOVER

There are three small clues. 'Scored' suggests 'counted' or 'calculated'. 'Contain' suggests there is a hidden message contained in the lines. 'Each line a greater than the one before' suggests counting incrementally.

180

Integrity - Solution

Trust **R**eflects **A**n **I**mage **T**wice **O**n **R**ested lovers' play
Reciprocating **A**ll **T**he while, faith being the faithful way
EXalted **L**ove, **O**ur **V**irtue's **E**nd, **R**ecycles its own clay

All **L**ove **I**nspires **A**lliance **R**ich, our bond a wealth we've earned
Close **H**earts **E**njoy **A** **T**rust well-taught and – in each kiss – re-learned
Honour **A**nd **R**omance **P**roclaim **Y**our love being mine returned

Each **V**iew **I** **L**ove is but of you, and how you lie with me
Reach **O**ut **T**o **T**his **E**ternal **N**eed for love's integrity
You **O**ffer **U**nderstanding's peace, which now, at last, I see

- - -

Key: Extract the initial letters from each line. These letters spell:

TREACHERY

In addition, in each line the initial letters of several words spell out various unkind and insulting terms:

Traitor
Rat
Ex-Lover
A Liar
Cheat
Harpy
Evil
Rotten
You

These nine insulting terms are not meant to form a coherent phrase. They are just meant to be nine words associated with the person being written about. I don't think the finished poem makes much sense but then again it's not meant to. It's meant to look like a rather pedestrian bit of verse vaguely pertaining to ideas of trust, fidelity and loyalty. It was difficult to compose. I probably tried about a hundred variations on each of the nine lines.

Infatuation – Solution

The summer sun we spent **A**s lovers do
Wrapped in the shaded **L**eisure of our care
But now these days of **I**dle dreams are through
As cooler rays draw **F**orth a calmer view
And gloomy clouds **E**clipse our sweet affair

Mourn as we may, no **T**ruth could be more clear
What we have had **I**s now a fading light
For all that we **M**ay share a fallen tear
To think upon **E**ach twilight kiss held dear
Time has run **O**ut on this impassioned flight

You told me **F**aithful love should never end
But I know **L**ove is just one season's play
The arts **O**f love we've shared do not depend
On arid **V**isions such as fools defend
Of one **I**nfatuation for all days

Thus **N**ow we part, let's not play or pretend
The **G**ood love goes, the tough love takes its place
To **Y**ou I say farewell my lover friend
I **O**ffer just one hope that I intend:
Use fewer letters and my wish you'll trace

- - -

Key: Take the 20th letter of line 1; the 19th letter of line 2; the 18th letter of line 3… and so on, all the way down to the 1st letter of line 20.

These letters spell

A LIFETIME OF LOVING YOU

In each case, the key letter is the start of a word *and* does not occur earlier in the same line. This is hard to achieve if the hidden phrase calls for a common letter such as 'e' to occur towards the end of a line. The composition of this poem was not without its difficulties.

I hope you enjoyed this book. I also hope you will recommend it to other people. Saying nice things about it online would help me enormously and I would be very grateful.

This is the sort of book that would make a nice gift for anyone getting married. It would also make a nice gift for anyone you like in a romantic way. Or for someone on Valentine's Day. Or for anyone who is in love or would like to be or has been. I suppose the point I'm making is that *every* man and woman in the world really ought to buy this book, either for themselves or as a gift.

— Ian Rowland

London, 2021

www.ianrowland.com
ian@ianrowland.com

Love, Thanks And Credits

Thanks to Francesca for doing such consistently wonderful illustrations; to her husband for all his support and for reciting some of my work; and their two lovely daughters.

Thanks to Lynne for being a truly magical friend who provides consistent support and encouragement as well as to Ambrose, Jade and all my friends in their respective communities.

Thanks to Andrew for legal support and guidance and to Lee and Paul for their proofreading services.

Thanks to the women who provided the material, stories and inspiration for this book and created some of the most magical chapters in my life. Also, thanks to my many friends who have, over the years, encouraged me to scribble things in the hope that I might one day write something worthwhile. Even though this hasn't happened yet, I appreciate the encouragement.

A Tribute To Francesca

I published the first edition of this book in 2013. At the time, the vague idea for what eventually became 'The Moon Carrier' had been rattling around in my head for about twelve years or so. The main reason for the delay was that I just couldn't find the right illustrator to work with. I had met a few talented illustrators from time to time but none seemed to have quite the right style I was looking for.

One day, quite by chance, Francesca DeWinter contacted me about an entirely unrelated matter. In the course of the conversation, she happened to mention that she did a little bit of illustration here and there and was looking for new projects to work on. Naturally, this piqued my interest. As soon as I saw some examples of Francesca's work, I knew that my search was over. I'd found the *perfect* illustrator to work with — someone who could help me bring 'The Moon Carrier' to life. After such a long and frustrating search, this felt like a very happy moment.

Collaborating with Francesca was a joy. Most of the time, we worked together via email. I sent her poems and suggested illustrations I thought it might be nice to have. Francesca sent me her notes about which poems she liked most (she was a very constructive critic) as well as her enchanting, magical and often very funny illustrations that never failed to delight me.

Francesca spared no effort to produce *exactly* the illustrations I wanted, even if this meant producing a dozen versions of an idea until it was *just* right. Time after time, I was stunned by her creative ingenuity. She tackled concepts such 'dragonflies playing helical chess' or 'cheese trying to master the cello' with great relish, proving that if I could write it, she'd find a way to draw it!

From time to time, we met up — most often at Brown's on St. Martin's Lane in London. Francesca brought her folders of ideas, sketches and finished drawings and we talked forever, happily working our way through afternoon tea followed by a few glasses of wine. Every so often, we remembered we were *supposed* to be discussing the book! On some occasions, we were joined by Francesca's husband Ian, a very successful actor and brilliantly entertaining company. They were memorably happy times. I felt privileged to spend time with two such very talented people.

Eventually, the work was complete and I published the book. Time passed, the world turned, seasons changed and I gradually lost touch with Francesca.

In 2021, while updating some of my other titles, I decided to produce a new edition of 'The Moon Carrier'. I emailed Francesca to ask a few purely technical questions. That's when I learned the terrible news from Ian: Francesca had passed away, taken from us long before her time by cancer. There are no words to express how cruel and tragic this is.

You can still see Francesca's superb work on her website: www.francescadewinter.com. While her site shows Francesca's radiant talent and brilliance, it cannot convey her warmth, her sparkling sense of fun and her generous, artistic spirit. I will never forget her or the joy, the delight, of our collaboration. I dedicate this book to her, to Ian and their two children.

Printed in Great Britain
by Amazon

86713117R00106